Contents

Week	Title	Page
	Preface	v

2009 Summer Training

**CRYSTALLIZATION-STUDY
OF
THE GOSPEL OF GOD**

	Title and Banners	135
7	The Structure of the Gospel of God—the Righteousness of God, the Life of Christ, and the Faith of the Believers	
	Outline	136
	Day 1	140
8	The Unsearchable Riches of Christ as the Gospel	
	Outline	155
	Day 1	160
9	The Mystery of the Gospel	
	Outline	174
	Day 1	178
10	Serving God in Our Spirit in the Gospel of His Son	
	Outline	192
	Day 1	198
11	The Faith as the Gospel and the Goal of the Gospel	
	Outline	213
	Day 1	218

Week	Title	Page
12	**The Genuine, Intrinsic, Highest, and Fullest Gospel of God's Economy**	
	Outline	233
	Day 1	238

Recovery Version Reading Schedules:
Old Testament   256
New Testament   256

Daily Verse Cards   261

The Holy Word for Morning Revival

Crystallization-Study of the Gospel of God

Volume Two

Witness Lee

Living Stream Ministry
Anaheim, CA • www.lsm.org

© 2009 Living Stream Ministry

All rights reserved. No part of this work may be reproduced or transmitted in any form or by any means—graphic, electronic, or mechanical, including photocopying, recording, or information storage and retrieval systems—without written permission from the publisher.

First Edition, August 2009.

ISBN 978-0-7363-4079-3

Published by

Living Stream Ministry

2431 W. La Palma Ave., Anaheim, CA 92801 U.S.A.
P. O. Box 2121, Anaheim, CA 92814 U.S.A.

Printed in the United States of America

09 10 11 12 13 / 6 5 4 3 2 1

Preface

1. This book is intended as an aid to believers in developing a daily time of morning revival with the Lord in His word. At the same time, it provides a limited review of the Summer Training held June 29—July 4, 2009, in Anaheim, California, on the "Crystallization-study of the Gospel of God." Through intimate contact with the Lord in His word, the believers can be constituted with life and truth and thereby equipped to prophesy in the meetings of the church unto the building up of the Body of Christ.
2. The entire content of this book is taken from the *Crystallization-study Outlines: The Gospel of God,* the text and footnotes of the Recovery Version of the Bible, selections from the writings of Witness Lee and Watchman Nee, and *Hymns,* all of which are published by Living Stream Ministry.
3. The book is divided into weeks. One training message is covered per week. Each week presents first the message outline, followed by six daily portions, a hymn, and then some space for writing. The training outline has been divided into days, corresponding to the six daily portions. Each daily portion covers certain points and begins with a section entitled "Morning Nourishment." This section contains selected verses and a short reading that can provide rich spiritual nourishment through intimate fellowship with the Lord. The "Morning Nourishment" is followed by a section entitled "Today's Reading," a longer portion of ministry related to the day's main points. Each day's portion concludes with a short list of references for further reading and some space for the saints to make notes concerning their spiritual inspiration, enlightenment, and enjoyment to serve as a reminder of what they have received of the Lord that day.
4. The space provided at the end of each week is for composing a short prophecy. This prophecy can be composed by considering all of our daily notes, the "harvest" of our

inspirations during the week, and preparing a main point with some sub-points to be spoken in the church meetings for the organic building up of the Body of Christ.

5. Following the last week in this volume, we have provided reading schedules for both the Old and New Testaments in the Recovery Version with footnotes. These schedules are arranged so that one can read through both the Old and New Testaments of the Recovery Version with footnotes in two years.

6. As a practical aid to the saints' feeding on the Word throughout the day, we have provided verse cards at the end of the volume, which correspond to each day's scripture reading. These may be cut out and carried along as a source of spiritual enlightenment and nourishment in the saints' daily lives.

7. The *Crystallization-study Outlines* were compiled by Living Stream Ministry from the writings of Witness Lee and Watchman Nee. The outlines, footnotes, and cross-references in the Recovery Version of the Bible are by Witness Lee. All of the other references cited in this publication are from the published ministry of Witness Lee and Watchman Nee.

Summer Training
(June 29—July 4, 2009)

CRYSTALLIZATION-STUDY OF THE GOSPEL OF GOD

Banners:

Set 1:

The gospel of God, the totality of the divine truths,
is the proclamation of Jesus Christ
according to the revelation of the mystery—
Christ as the mystery of God
and the church as the mystery of Christ.

The gospel of Christ as the threefold seed in humanity—
the seed of the woman, the seed of Abraham,
and the seed of David—
is the good news of the revelation of the entire Bible.

The gospel of God is the gospel of the kingdom of God,
which brings us under the rule of God's authority,
and the gospel of the glory of Christ, which illuminates,
radiates, and shines into our hearts.

Our service to God, our worship to God,
is by the Spirit of God in our spirit in the gospel of His Son,
and the issue of this service, this worship,
is the reality of the Body of Christ.

Set 2:

The genuine, intrinsic, highest, and fullest gospel
is the gospel of God's economy—the gospel of sonship
for the building up of the church as the Body of Christ
by the building of God into man and man into God.

The goal of the gospel is that,
loving the Lord Jesus with the first love,
we would pour out upon Him what is most precious to us,
even our most costly and valuable spiritual treasure,
"wasting" ourselves upon Him.

WEEK 7 — OUTLINE

The Structure of the Gospel of God— the Righteousness of God, the Life of Christ, and the Faith of the Believers

Scripture Reading: Rom. 1:16-17; 3:22; 5:1-11; 10:17; Heb. 11:1; 12:1-2a

Day 1
I. The key word concerning the gospel of God in Romans and the banner of God's eternal economy is Romans 1:17, which reveals the structure of the gospel of God—"the <u>righteous</u> shall have <u>life</u> and live by <u>faith</u>."

II. The righteousness of God is the procedure of God's salvation judicially (vv. 16-17):
   A. God cannot forgive sinful people without meeting the demands of His righteousness (Psa. 103:6-7); according to His righteousness, "the soul who sins, he shall die" (Ezek. 18:4) and "the wages of sin is death" (Rom. 6:23):
      1. Christ died a vicarious death as the Substitute for sinners, a death that was legal according to God's law and was recognized and approved by God according to the law (Isa. 53:5-6; 2 Cor. 5:21; Matt. 27:45-46).
      2. Christ, the righteous One, was judged on behalf of us, the unrighteous, by the righteous God according to His righteousness, that He might remove the barrier of our sins and bring us to God (1 Pet. 3:18).
      3. On the cross Jesus was made sin for us, condemned sin in the flesh, and by dying on our behalf fulfilled all God's righteousness; now for the sake of His righteousness, God must forgive us (2 Cor. 5:21; Rom. 8:3, 10; John 19:30).

Day 2
   B. Because God is bound by His righteousness to forgive us, righteousness is the power of God's salvation and the unshakable foundation of our salvation (Rom. 1:16-17):
      1. Our experience of Christ rests on the foundation

of God's righteousness, which is the solid, steadfast, and unshakable foundation of His throne (Psa. 89:14) and the base on which His kingdom is built (Rom. 14:17).
   2. God has put Christ to death on our behalf, He has recognized the death of Christ as the full payment of our debt of sins, and the resurrected and ascended Christ sitting at the right hand of God is the "receipt" of this payment (4:24-25).
   3. Thus, whenever we claim the blood of Jesus and appeal to God's righteousness, He has no choice except to forgive us (1 John 1:9; *Hymns,* #1003).
  C. Life is the goal of God's salvation; thus, justification is "of life"; through justification we have come up to the standard of God's righteousness and correspond with it so that now He can impart His life into us (Rom. 5:18).
III. **The life of Christ is the purpose of God's salvation organically (v. 10):**
  A. The result of our justification is the full enjoyment of God in Christ as our life; in God's organic salvation we have love, grace, peace, hope, life, glory, the Holy Spirit, Christ, and God as our enjoyment (vv. 1-11).
  B. The saving life of Christ is accomplishing the organic goal of God's dynamic salvation in the following ways (v. 10):
   1. We have been justified by God in Christ as the righteousness from God to us so that we may live in this life before God (1:17).
   2. This life makes the God-justified believers the many sons of God (8:14; Heb. 2:10), who are the many brothers of Christ (Rom. 8:29) through regeneration (1 Pet. 1:3) by the Spirit of life (Rom. 8:2) with God's producing and multiplying life.
   3. This life is imparted into the dying believers so that they may grow in Christ out of death unto maturity (v. 11).
   4. The indwelling Christ moves in the believers

by the Spirit of life so that they may enjoy Christ's life with its peace (vv. 5-6).
5. This life sanctifies us with the holy nature of God as the holy element (6:19-20).
6. This life renews us, by the Spirit of life, based upon the washing of regeneration, from the old element of our old man into the new constitution of our new man (12:2b; Titus 3:5).
7. This life transforms us metabolically by the Spirit of life with the element of Christ's divine life, from our old constitution to our new constitution, for the building up of Christ's organic Body (Rom. 12:2b, 5; 2 Cor. 3:18).
8. This life conforms us to the image of Christ as the firstborn Son of God so that we may be full-grown God-men for the Triune God's expression (Rom. 8:29).
9. This life glorifies us through the redemption of our body so that we may enter into the freedom of glory and our full sonship (vv. 21, 23, 30).
10. This life makes us reign as kings over Satan, sin, and death (5:17, 21).
11. All the above ten items are for the producing and building up of the organic Body of Christ expressed as the local churches; this is covered in the last five chapters of the book of Romans.

Day 4 & Day 5

IV. **The faith of the believers is the substantiation of God's salvation practically (Heb. 11:1):**
   A. The faith of the believers is actually not their own faith but Christ entering into them to be their faith (Rom. 1:12; 3:22 and footnote 1; Gal. 2:16 and footnote 1).
   B. Our believing into Christ is our appreciation of Him as a reaction to His attraction (Rom. 10:17; Heb. 12:1-2a; cf. Acts 14:27).
   C. Faith comes out of the hearing of the word; when we come to the living Word (Christ) in the written word (the Bible), He becomes the applied word (the

Spirit) of faith to us (Rom. 10:8, 17; Gal. 3:2; cf. Heb. 3:12).
D. When man hears Christ, knows Him, appreciates Him, and treasures Him, He causes faith to be generated in man, becoming the faith in man that enables man to believe in Him (12:2a; Rom. 10:17; Gal. 3:2, 5; 5:6).
E. Faith is to believe that God is and we are not; He must be the only One, the unique One, in everything, and we must be nothing in everything (Heb. 11:1, 5-6).

Day 6
F. As believers, we live by faith and infuse Christ as faith into others by exercising our spirit of faith (2 Cor. 4:13; Rom. 10:14-17; Acts 26:22-29) so that they may be brought into the following organic relationships with Christ for His purpose:
 1. Christ is the cultivated olive tree and the vine, and we are His branches (Rom. 11:17, 24; John 15:1-8).
 2. Christ is the Head, and we are His members (1 Cor. 12:12, 27).
 3. Christ is the breath of life, the water of life, and the bread of life, and we are His breathers, drinkers, and eaters (John 20:22; 4:10, 14; 7:37-39a; 6:35, 51-63, 68).
 4. Christ is the Bridegroom, and we are His bride (3:29-30; 2 Cor. 11:2-3).
G. Faith is the subjective God applied to our being; thus, just as nothing is impossible to God, nothing is impossible to faith (Matt. 17:20; 19:26).
H. The great irrepressible and unlimited power of faith motivates thousands to suffer for the Lord, risk their lives, and become overcoming sent ones and martyrs to spread the gospel of God's eternal economy unto the uttermost part of the earth (Luke 18:8; Rom. 16:3-4; Acts 20:24; 1 Tim. 1:4, 11-12; Matt. 24:14; Acts 1:8).

WEEK 7 — DAY 1

Morning Nourishment

Rom. 1:16-17 ...The gospel...is the power of God unto salvation to everyone who believes....For the righteousness of God is revealed in it out of faith to faith, as it is written, "But the righteous shall have life and live by faith."

1 Pet. 3:18 For Christ also has suffered once for sins, the Righteous on behalf of the unrighteous, that He might bring you to God...

Now...we want to see the structure of the gospel of God. All the parts of this structure are mentioned in Romans 1:17....It says, "The righteous shall have life and live by faith." This is the key word concerning the gospel of God in the book of Romans. In this verse there are *righteousness, life,* and *faith*. Righteousness is of God, life is of Christ, and faith is of the believers....The gospel of God is built up with these three parts. Romans first shows us the righteousness of God judicially. Then it shows us the life of Christ organically. Third, it shows us the faith of the believers practically. According to...the book of Romans, the structure of the gospel of God is of the righteousness of God, the life of Christ, and the faith of the believers. (*Crystallization-study of the Epistle to the Romans*, p. 48)

Today's Reading

The ***righteous*** shall have ***life*** and live by ***faith!*** This word should be the banner of God's eternal economy, which is altogether a matter in faith (1 Tim. 1:4)!

The righteous, those who are absolutely right before God and before man, shall have life, the divine life. Then, how can we, the vile sinners, have the divine life of the righteous God according to His righteousness? By faith! It is by faith, which is the moving and working God in Christ who puts us into Christ as our righteousness (1 Cor. 1:30), that we, the sinners, have the divine life according to God's righteousness judicially. By this linking faith we are linked to God in Christ to participate in all that the all-inclusive Christ is, has, and has attained to, for the producing of the organic members of Christ to constitute and build up His organic Body, which will consummate in the New Jerusalem as the enlargement

WEEK 7 — DAY 1

and expression of the eternal Triune God in His unlimited glory in the mysterious mingling of divinity with humanity for eternity (Rev. 21:2—22:5). This is the eternal fulfillment of the gospel in Romans 1:17, that "the righteous shall have life and live by faith"! (*Crystallization-study of the Epistle to the Romans*, pp. 123-124)

In eternity past God predestinated us to be His sons. However, although we were the predestinated ones, we became fallen and involved with sin. This brings in the matter of God's righteousness. If we had not fallen, we would not need to be concerned with righteousness. But because we are fallen, God must deal with us according to His righteousness. What should God do with those He has predestinated to become His sons? Some may say that because God loves us, He cannot cast us all into the lake of fire. Yes, God loves us, but He hates sin. God does not desire to give us up or to cast us into the lake of fire. However, He cannot forgive us unless His righteousness has been satisfied. If God would forgive us in a light manner, He would place Himself in a position of being unrighteous. As a righteous God and a just God, He cannot forgive sinful people without meeting the demands of His righteousness.

In order that God might be able to forgive us, Christ, the Son of God, became flesh. As Romans 8:3 says, God sent His own Son in the likeness of the flesh of sin. By incarnation, the Lord took upon Himself the likeness of the flesh of sin and became identified with sinners in the flesh. For the sake of God's righteousness, the Lord Jesus was put to death on the cross. There, on the cross, He was made sin for us, and God condemned sin in the flesh. By dying on our behalf the Lord accomplished redemption and fulfilled all of God's righteous requirements. Now God has the position righteously to forgive us. In fact, He not only can forgive us, but, for the sake of His righteousness, He must forgive us. God forgives not primarily because He loves us, but because He is bound by His righteousness to do so. (*Life-study of Romans*, pp. 597-598)

Further Reading: Crystallization-study of the Epistle to the Romans, msgs. 5, 11

Enlightenment and inspiration: _____

WEEK 7 — DAY 2

Morning Nourishment

Rom. 4:24-25 ...Jesus our Lord...who was delivered for our offenses and was raised for our justification.

1 John 1:9 If we confess our sins, He is faithful and righteous to forgive us our sins and cleanse us from all unrighteousness.

The book of Romans...reveals that we are saved not by grace nor by love, but by righteousness. Neither love nor grace is a legal matter. You cannot claim that, according to law, a person is required to love you or to show grace to you. Only with those things which are related to righteousness do we have the position to claim something in a legal way.

The requirements of God's righteousness had been fulfilled by Christ's death, and God was satisfied. Three days later, as proof of this satisfaction, God raised Christ from among the dead. Hence, the resurrection of Christ is the proof that God is satisfied with His death on our behalf.

Before Christ died on the cross, it was still possible for God to change His mind about forgiving us of our sins. He could righteously have cast us all aside. But after Christ's death on the cross under the judgment of God, God cannot do this.

Both love and grace may change, but righteousness is solid and steadfast. God is free either to love us or not to love us. However, He is bound by His righteousness. Now that Christ has died to fulfill God's righteous requirements, God has put Himself into a position where He is legally bound. Whether He loves us or not, He is bound by His own righteousness to forgive us. Thus, the foundation of our salvation is righteousness, not love or grace. Psalm 89:14 says, "Righteousness and justice are the foundation of Your throne." The very foundation of God's throne is also the foundation of our salvation. (*Life-study of Romans,* pp. 598-600)

Today's Reading

The Bible does not say that love is the power of the gospel; neither does it say that grace is the power of the gospel. But it does reveal that the righteousness of God is the power of the gospel. If we consider ourselves, we shall realize that we are not lovable nor worthy of God's grace. We simply do not deserve anything from God. But God is righteous. He put Christ to death on our behalf, and He has recognized the death of Christ as the full payment of our debt. Furthermore, the resurrected Christ sitting at God's right hand is the receipt of payment. Since God has already issued this receipt, how could He righteously claim payment again from us?

We can boldly tell God, "If You don't deal with me according to Your righteousness, Your throne will be shaken. The important issue is not whether I shall be saved or perish; it is whether or not You will allow the foundation of Your throne to be shaken. God, for me to perish is a secondary matter. The primary matter is the righteous foundation of Your throne. God, I remind You of Your righteousness. Christ has died for my sins, and He is now at Your right hand as proof that You have received His payment of all my debts. According to Your righteousness, You have no choice except to save me. Christ has died, You have accepted His death and have resurrected Him from among the dead, and now You are legally bound to forgive me. By resurrecting Christ You indicated that You were satisfied with His payment and You issued a receipt of payment. O God, if You were not satisfied with Christ, then You should have allowed Him to remain in the tomb. O Father God, I appreciate Your love and Your grace. But now I stand before You not so much in love or in grace, but in Your righteousness. Now, no matter what my condition is, You must forgive me."

It pleases God whenever someone prays like this. This is a prayer that appeals to God according to His righteousness. The gospel of Christ is the power of God because the righteousness of God is revealed in it.

Whenever we claim the blood of Jesus and appeal to God's righteousness, God has no choice except to forgive us (1 John 1:9). (*Life-study of Romans,* pp. 600-601, 603)

Further Reading: Life-study of Romans, msg. 57

Enlightenment and inspiration: _____
_____
_____
_____

WEEK 7 — DAY 3

Morning Nourishment

Rom. For if we, being enemies, were reconciled to God
5:10 through the death of His Son, much more we will be saved in His life, having been reconciled.
 17 For if, by the offense of the one, death reigned through the one, much more those who receive the abundance of grace and of the gift of righteousness will reign in life through the One, Jesus Christ.
8:29 Because those whom He foreknew, He also predestinated *to be* conformed to the image of His Son, that He might be the Firstborn among many brothers.

The second section of God's full salvation is the section of consummation by the life of Christ organically as the completion of God's salvation....Now we want to see what the life of Christ, as the continuation of God's building, has accomplished for us.

First, it gives the believing sinners life, who have been justified by God in Christ as the righteousness from God to them that they may live in this life before God (Rom. 1:17).

Also, this life makes the God-justified believers the many sons of God (Rom. 8:14; Heb. 2:10), who are the many brothers of Christ (Rom. 8:29) through regeneration (1 Pet. 1:3) by the Spirit of life (Rom. 8:2) with Christ's producing and multiplying life.

This life is imparted into the dying believers that they may grow in Christ out of death unto maturity (Rom. 8:11). Our regeneration transpired in our spirit. But we have another part of our being which is dying, that is, our mortal body. We need the life of Christ to be dispensed into this dying part. (*Crystallization-study of the Epistle to the Romans,* pp. 63-64)

Today's Reading

The indwelling Christ moves in the believers by the Spirit of life that they may enjoy Christ's life with its peace (Rom. 8:5-6). People who gamble set their mind on gambling, but our mind is set on the spirit. We can set our mind on the spirit because the indwelling pneumatic Christ is moving in us. The result is that we have Christ's life with peace.

Another accomplishment of the life of Christ in God's dynamic salvation is that it sanctifies us (Rom. 6:19-20) with the holy nature of God as the holy element.

This life renews us, by the Spirit of life, based upon the washing of regeneration, from the old element of our old man into the new constitution of our new man (Rom. 12:2b; Titus 3:5).

It also transforms us metabolically by the Spirit of life with the element of Christ's divine life, from our old constitution to our new constitution, for the building up of Christ's organic Body (Rom. 12:2b, 5; 2 Cor. 3:18).

This life goes on to conform us to the image of Christ as the firstborn Son of God that we may be the full-grown God-men for the Triune God's expression (Rom. 8:29).

Such a life glorifies us through the redemption of our body that we may enter into the freedom of glory and our full sonship (Rom. 8:21, 23, 30). Although we are sons of God, many times we are weak because of our mortal body. But one day our body will be glorified and redeemed. We will be the glorious sons of God, who can soar like an eagle. Isaiah 40:31 says, "Yet those who wait on Jehovah will renew their strength; / They will mount up with wings like eagles." In the coming age, when our bodies are redeemed, we will be able to fly like the transcendent, soaring birds.

The life of Christ in which we are saved also makes us reign as kings mainly over the negative things such as Satan, sin, the world, the flesh, etc.

All the above ten items are for the producing and the building up of the organic Body of Christ expressed as the local churches; this is covered in the last five chapters of the book of Romans. (*Crystallization-study of the Epistle to the Romans,* pp. 64-65)

Further Reading: Crystallization-study of the Epistle to the Romans, msg. 6; *Life-study of Romans,* msg. 9

Enlightenment and inspiration: _____
_____
_____

WEEK 7 — DAY 4

Morning Nourishment

Rom. 3:22 Even the righteousness of God through the faith of Jesus Christ to all those who believe, for there is no distinction.

10:8 ..."The word is near you, in your mouth and in your heart," that is, the word of the faith which we proclaim.

17 So faith *comes* out of hearing, and hearing through the word of Christ.

The faith of the believers is actually not their own faith but Christ entering into them to be their faith (Rom. 3:22 and footnote 1; Gal. 2:16 and footnote 1). Now we need to consider how and when Christ entered into us to be our faith. When we repented unto God, the pneumatic Christ as the sanctifying Spirit of God (1 Pet. 1:2a) moved within us to be our faith by which we believed on the Lord Jesus (Acts 16:31). Romans 10:17 says, "So faith comes out of hearing, and hearing through the word of Christ." As sinners we did not have faith. Faith came into us by our hearing the word. This word is just Christ Himself.

When we heard the gospel, the preacher described Christ to us. The more we heard, the more we saw Christ and were attracted to Christ....The preachers preach Christ to present Christ's beauty. After hearing such a word about Christ, that is, after seeing such a Christ, within you there is an appreciation of Christ, and your appreciation of Him is the reaction to His attraction. We can believe in the Lord Jesus because we hear about Him, that is, we see Him. We read the Bible, and in the Bible we see something about Him. (*Crystallization-study of the Epistle to the Romans*, pp. 69-70)

Today's Reading

According to Romans 10:17, faith comes out of the hearing of the word. Thus, the source of faith is the word, but we have to realize the crystallization of this point. There are three aspects of the word. First, there is the written word of God—the Bible (John 10:35). Then there is the living Word of God—Christ (John 1:1). Finally, there is the applied word of God—the Spirit (Eph. 6:17; John 6:63).

The Bible is the written word, and Christ is the living Word.

Without the Spirit, however, the living Word cannot be applied to us. The living Word becomes the applied word through the Spirit.

If you have the opportunity, it would be very good to preach the gospel according to this crystallization of Romans. Tell people about Christ in His divinity and humanity, in His being the only begotten Son of God and the firstborn Son of God. Many logical and thoughtful people would be attracted to such a wonderful person in the universe. Try in your vital group to go out to touch people by presenting Christ in the way that you have heard in these messages. After seeing, that is, after knowing, such a Christ, who would not believe in Him? Faith comes from hearing, hearing equals seeing, and seeing equals knowing Christ. Faith comes from hearing, and hearing is from the word of Christ.

When the proper preaching of the gospel is going on, the Spirit, the pneumatic Christ, accompanies that preaching. That preaching speaks Christ outside of you, but the pneumatic Christ right away accompanies that preaching and works within you. Then you repent and appreciate such a One. Spontaneously something within you rises up. This is your faith, your believing. Your believing comes from your knowing of Christ. Your believing actually is your appreciation of Christ as a reaction to His attraction. Only the believers, not the sinners, have this kind of reaction.

If you see this point, you will say, "Lord Jesus, even my believing in You is You Yourself. You are so attractive and beauteous! Who can help but believe in You?" Many young people have been attracted by the Savior's beauty. Even if their parents persecute them and threaten them to death, they will not give up their faith in Christ. This kind of faith is Christ Himself. By such a faith the believing ones believe that God raised Jesus Christ from the dead that they may be saved (Rom. 10:9b-10a; 5:1). They have access through faith into the grace in which they now stand (Rom. 5:2). (*Crystallization-study of the Epistle to the Romans*, pp. 83, 70-71)

Further Reading: Crystallization-study of the Epistle to the Romans, msg. 7

Enlightenment and inspiration: _____
_____
_____
_____

Morning Nourishment

Heb. 11:1 Now faith is the substantiation of things hoped for, the conviction of things not seen.

5-6 By faith Enoch...was not found, because God had translated him. For...he obtained the testimony that he had been well pleasing to God. But without faith it is impossible to be well pleasing *to Him*, for he who comes forward to God must believe that He is and that He is a rewarder of those who diligently seek Him.

He who comes forward to God must believe that God is (Heb. 11:6b). This is very simple. God requires you only to believe that He is. The verb *to be* is actually the divine title of our Triune God. In Exodus 3 Moses asked God what His name was. God answered that His name is I Am That I Am (vv. 13-14). Our God's name is the verb *to be*. He is "I Am That I Am." He is the only One.

We must believe that God is. This implies everything. Do you need God? God is. Do you need food? God is. This is why we use the word *great* in saying that Jesus is the *great* I Am. He told us, "I am...the life" (John 14:6a), "I am the resurrection" (11:25), "I am the door" (10:7, 9), "I am the good Shepherd" (10:11), "I am the bread of life" (6:35). He is the real food. There is only one kind of food that is. This food is Jesus, the great I Am. He is the breath (20:22), the living water (4:10, 14), and the tree of life (15:1; 14:6a; Rev. 2:7). He is God (John 1:1; 20:28-29; Rom. 9:5), the Father (Isa. 9:6; John 14:9-10), the Son (Mark 1:1; John 20:31), and the Spirit (2 Cor. 3:17; 1 Cor. 15:45b). He is everything to us. (*Crystallization-study of the Epistle to the Romans,* pp. 73-74)

Today's Reading

The Bible says that if you do not believe in Christ, you have no life (John 3:15-16, 36). When I was young, I could not understand this. I thought that as a strong boy, I did have life. Later, I realized that our life is a false one. It is not the life that is. This means that our life is not something that exists forever. We are today, but eventually we will not be tomorrow. So in the whole universe, we are nothing. I am nothing. Our hall is nothing. Anaheim is nothing. California is nothing. The United States is nothing. And the whole globe is nothing! This is because they do not exist forever. The day will come when they will not exist; they will be over. Actually, the things that are seen are not the things that exist; they are vanities (2 Cor. 4:18).

Then what is existing? Who exists? Only the great I Am—I Am That I Am. He who comes forward to God must believe that God is! Faith is so critical. Without this, you can never make God happy. You must believe that God is. Let me illustrate. If a husband realized that only God is and he is not, then he would not love his wife by himself and in himself.

What is faith? Faith is to stop yourself from doing anything. You are nothing. Faith joins you with God to make God the only One who is. I am not, so I should not be the one who loves my wife. It should be Christ loving my wife. He is; I am not.

Faith is to stop you from doing anything but to make God everything to you. This equals Paul's word in Galatians 2:20: "I am crucified with Christ; and it is no longer I who live, but it is Christ who lives in me." Who lives? It is no longer I. I do not exist. I was terminated. I was crucified. I am finished. It is no more I, but Christ lives in me. Christ lives. Christ is. Christ exists. I do not exist. This is the very essence of the short word *believe that God is*. To believe that God is implies that you are not. He must be the only One, the unique One, in everything, and we must be nothing in everything.

Only faith can make God happy....To deny yourself and to trust in Him is faith. This is to believe that God is.

Even at the end of a ministry meeting, we may say, "Saints, now it is your turn to share." But we have to say, "It is not our turn, but Christ's turn." If we live in this way, the riches of Christ will come out of our mouth. This makes a big difference—to deny the self, to trust in the Lord, that is, to believe that God is. (*Crystallization-study of the Epistle to the Romans,* pp. 74-75, 77-78)

Further Reading: Crystallization-study of the Epistle to the Romans, msg. 7

Enlightenment and inspiration: _____
_____
_____

WEEK 7 — DAY 6

Morning Nourishment

Rom. 4:17 ...In the sight of God whom [Abraham] believed, who gives life to the dead and calls the things not being as being.

Matt. 17:20 ...If you have faith like a mustard seed, you will say to this mountain, Move from here to there, and it will move; and nothing will be impossible to you.

The source of faith is God. He is the One who calls things not being as being and gives life to the dead (Rom. 4:17). In Genesis 1, there was no light, so God said, "Let there be light," and light was there (v. 3). We are related to God through these three aspects of His word: the written word, the living word, and the applied word. Then we enjoy God as the One who calls not being as being and who gives life to the dead. Nothing is impossible to faith (see *Hymns,* #535), because faith is actually God Himself.

The more of God you have, the more faith you have. We can gain God by coming to the Bible, the written word. But if we merely read the Bible, it could only be the dead letter to us. Before reading the Bible, it is good to call on the Lord at least two or three times, "O Lord Jesus. O Lord Jesus." Right away, the written word of the Bible becomes the living word. That is Christ. Then we react to Him, and He becomes the word as the Spirit, the word applied by the Spirit. Then we have God. God is added into our being, and this God is the source of faith.

The God who calls not being as being and who gives life to the dead is embodied in Christ. Whenever you have God, you have His embodiment, and His embodiment is Christ. This embodiment is realized in the Spirit. So the faith is the faith of God, the faith of Christ (Gal. 2:20, 16; 3:22, 26; Rom. 3:22), and the faith of the Spirit. Thus, the faith is the faith of the embodied and realized Triune God. (*Crystallization-study of the Epistle to the Romans,* pp. 84-85)

Today's Reading

The crystallization of faith is to believe that God is. The crystallization of the source of faith is God in His written word contacted as the living word and applied as the word of the Spirit so that we can gain the Triune God, who is able to call not being as being and give life to the dead. This One is embodied in Christ and realized in the Spirit. So faith is the Triune God embodied and realized. God in the written word becomes the living word applied as the word of the Spirit. Thus, God embodied in Christ and realized in the Spirit is faith.

In Matthew 17:20b the Lord spoke concerning the effect of faith: "If you have faith like a mustard seed, you will say to this mountain, Move from here to there, and it will move; and nothing will be impossible to you." Nothing is impossible to faith. *Hymns,* #535, written by Charles Wesley, expresses this effect of faith.

Only God is all-able, omnipotent; nothing is impossible to Him (Matt. 19:26). But the Lord also indicates that nothing is impossible to faith. So this indicates faith and God, God and faith, are one. If you do not have God, God remains apart from you. If you have God in you, this God becomes faith. Faith is the subjective God applied to your being. Thus, just as nothing is impossible to God, nothing is impossible to faith.

The believers are the believing ones in Christ, who are the household of faith (Gal. 6:10). In the universe there are many houses with many households. But there is one particular house with millions of members. That is the house of faith. We belong to this house. This is a big family, and the family name is *faith*. This is the home of faith. We may say that a certain home is the Smith home or the Lee home. Now we are all members of the "faith home."

This faith house is a house that believes in God through His word. Hebrews 1 says that God has spoken (v. 2). This word becomes the living word, Christ, and this living word is applied by the Spirit. Then we have the Triune God as the word in us.

The believers' faith in Christ brings them into the life union with Christ (John 3:15, 36). (*Crystallization-study of the Epistle to the Romans,* pp. 85-87)

Further Reading: Crystallization-study of the Epistle to the Romans, msgs. 8-10

Enlightenment and inspiration: _____

Hymns, #535

1. All things are possible to him
That can in Jesus' name believe;
Lord, I no more Thy name blaspheme,
Thy truth I lovingly receive.
I can, I do believe in Thee;
All things are possible to me.

2. 'Twas most impossible of all
That here sin's reign in me should cease;
Yet shall it be, I know it shall;
Jesus, I trust Thy faithfulness.
If nothing is too hard for Thee,
All things are possible to me.

3. Though earth and hell the Word gainsay,
The Word of God shall never fail;
The Lord can break sin's iron sway;
'Tis certain, though impossible.
The thing impossible shall be,
All things are possible to me.

4. All things are possible to God;
To Christ, the power of God in man;
To me when I am all renewed,
In Christ am fully formed again,
And from the reign of sin set free,
All things are possible to me.

5. All things are possible to God;
To Christ, the power of God in me;
Now shed Thy mighty Self abroad,
Let me no longer live, but Thee;
Give me this hour in Thee to prove
The sweet omnipotence of love.

WEEK 7 — PROPHECY

Composition for prophecy with main point and sub-points:

WEEK 8 — OUTLINE

The Unsearchable Riches of Christ as the Gospel

Scripture Reading: Eph. 3:8; 1 Cor. 1:9, 30; 2:2; 4:1-2; 2 Cor. 4:7; Deut. 8:7-10; Col. 1:12; 2:6-7a

Day 1

I. The apostle Paul enjoyed and announced the person of Christ with His unsearchable riches as the gospel to produce the church as the fullness of Christ, the expression and overflow of Christ, for the exhibition of Christ as the multifarious wisdom of God according to the eternal plan of God (Eph. 3:8-11, 16-19; 1:22-23; Acts 17:3, 18; 26:22a, 23; 13:47; Gal. 1:15a, 16a; Phil. 1:18; Col. 1:27b-28; 1 Cor. 1:24, 30).

II. In our living and serving, we should concentrate on enjoying and ministering Christ to dispense Him into others as the unique treasure of untold wealth in the universe, not on any persons, matters, or things other than Christ (vv. 9, 30; 2:2; 4:1-2; 2 Cor. 3:3, 6; 4:7):

Day 2

A. The proper preaching of Jesus as the glad tidings, the gospel, causes people to realize that they are nothing and that Christ is everything (Isa. 40:15, 17; cf. Phil. 3:7-8).

B. Our Savior, Jesus, is the Holy One, the eternal God, Jehovah, and the Creator of the heavens and the earth, who sits above the circle of the earth; as the Holy One, Jesus is unlimited, unsearchable, incomparable, and high (Isa. 40:12-15, 17-18, 22, 25-26, 28; Rom. 1:20; 11:34; Col. 1:15-18; Heb. 1:2-3; 11:1-3):

1. The way to enjoy the unsearchably rich Christ is to take Him as our real Sabbath rest, stopping ourselves with our living, doing, and activity, and receive Him as our life, person, and replacement; then we will experience Christ as the power of resurrection to be transformed and to soar in the heavens far above

WEEK 8 — OUTLINE

every earthly frustration (Matt. 11:28-30; Isa. 40:28-31).

2. God wants us to stop our doing, be replaced by Christ, and keep away from the taste of anything other than Christ (Gal. 2:20; John 6:57; Isa. 55:1-2; 58:3).

C. Christ Himself is our unsearchably rich portion and inheritance; our reward for our priestly service is to eat Christ and enjoy Him as everything to us (Num. 18:20, 31; John 6:57; Gen. 15:1; Psa. 43:4a; Phil. 3:8-9, 14):

1. We can enjoy the riches of Christ by calling on His name—the Lord is "rich to all who call upon Him; for 'whoever calls upon the name of the Lord shall be saved'" (Rom. 10:12b-13).

2. We can enjoy the riches of Christ in His word—we live on "every word that proceeds out through the mouth of God" (Matt. 4:4).

Day 3

3. We can enjoy the bountiful supply of the Body of Christ and His universal dimensions when we abide in Christ as our prison to live Him for His magnification and to receive God's visions and heavenly expressions on behalf of the saints (Phil. 1:19-21a; Eph. 3:1, 16-18; 4:1).

4. We can enjoy the treasure of His indwelling presence by loving Him in the midst of consuming pressures and tribulations, which are the sweet visitation and incarnation of grace for the God of resurrection to add Himself to us (2 Cor. 4:7; 1:8-9, 12; 12:7-10; Rom. 5:3; 8:28).

III. **The unsearchable riches of Christ as the gospel are revealed in all twenty-seven books of the New Testament; this wonderful, heavenly Christ is the very embodiment of the processed Triune God, reaching us as the consummated life-giving Spirit, so that we can continually receive Him as grace upon grace to be renewed day by day for serving our God in newness of spirit in the gospel of His Son**

WEEK 8 — OUTLINE

(John 1:14, 16; 1 Cor. 15:45b; 2 Cor. 4:16; Rom. 1:9; 7:6):

A. In the Gospels is the Christ who lived on the earth and died on the cross for the accomplishment of redemption.
B. In the Acts is the resurrected and ascended Christ propagated and ministered to men.
C. In Romans is the Christ who is our righteousness for justification and our life for sanctification, transformation, conformation, glorification, and building up.
D. In Galatians is the Christ who enables us to live a life that is versus the law, religion, tradition, and forms.
E. In Philippians is the Christ who is lived out of His members.
F. In Ephesians and Colossians is the Christ who is the life, the content, and the Head of the Body, the church.
G. In 1 and 2 Corinthians is the Christ who is everything in the practical church life.
H. In 1 and 2 Thessalonians is the Christ who is our holiness for His coming back.
I. In 1 and 2 Timothy and Titus is the Christ who is God's economy, enabling us to know how to conduct ourselves in the house of God.
J. In Hebrews is the present Christ, who is now in the heavens as our Minister and our High Priest, ministering to us the heavenly life, grace, authority, and power and sustaining us to live a heavenly life on earth.
K. In the Epistles of Peter is the Christ who enables us to take God's governmental dealings administered through sufferings.
L. In the Epistles of John is the Christ who is the life and fellowship of the children of God in God's family.
M. In Revelation is the Christ who is walking among the churches in this age, ruling over the world in the kingdom in the coming age, and expressing God in

WEEK 8 — OUTLINE

full glory in the new heaven and new earth for eternity.

N. Such a wonderful, all-inclusive, all-extensive, and universally rich Christ is the Christ now, the Christ today, and the Christ on the throne in the heavens, who is our daily salvation and moment-by-moment supply (Heb. 8:2; 4:14-16; 7:26; Rom. 5:10).

Day 4

IV. **God's goal in His economy is not merely to redeem His people and save them from the world, typified by Egypt, but to bring them into Christ, typified by the good land, so that they may possess Him and enjoy His unsearchable riches (Exo. 3:8; Deut. 8:7-10; Col. 1:12; 2:6-7a; Eph. 3:8):**

A. The riches of the good land typify the unsearchable riches of Christ in different aspects as the bountiful supply of the Spirit to His believers (Deut. 8:7-9):
1. The waterbrooks, springs, and fountains signify Christ as the flowing Spirit (John 4:14; 7:37-39; Rev. 22:1).
2. The valleys and the mountains signify the different kinds of environments in which we may experience Christ as the flowing Spirit (cf. 2 Cor. 6:8-10).

Day 5

3. Wheat typifies the incarnated Christ, who was crucified and buried to multiply Himself (John 12:24), and barley, being the first-ripe grain (2 Sam. 21:9), points to the resurrected Christ as the firstfruits (1 Cor. 15:20).
4. Vines typify the Christ who sacrificed Himself to produce wine to cheer God and man (Judg. 9:13; Matt. 9:17).
5. The fig tree speaks of the sweetness and satisfaction of Christ as the life supply (Judg. 9:11).
6. The pomegranates signify the fullness, the abundance and beauty, and the expression of the riches of Christ as life (Exo. 28:33-34; 1 Kings 7:18-20; S. S. 4:3b, 13).

Day 6

7. The olive tree typifies Christ (Rom. 11:17, 24) as the One who was filled with the Spirit and anointed with the Spirit (Luke 4:1, 18; Heb. 1:9); olive oil typifies the Holy Spirit, by whom we walk to honor God and whom we minister to honor man (Gal. 5:16, 25; 2 Cor. 3:6, 8; Judg. 9:9).
8. Milk and honey speak forth the goodness and sweetness of Christ (Deut. 6:3; Exo. 3:8).
9. Stones signify Christ as material for building God's dwelling place (Isa. 28:16; Zech. 4:7; 1 Pet. 2:4).
10. The iron and copper are for making weapons (Gen. 4:22; 1 Sam. 17:5-7) and typify our spiritual warfare by which we fight the enemy (2 Cor. 10:4; Eph. 6:10-20); iron also signifies Christ's ruling authority (Matt. 28:18; Rev. 19:15), and copper, Christ's judging power (1:15); the mountains from which copper is mined signify Christ's resurrection and ascension (Eph. 4:8).

B. By enjoying the riches of the land, the children of Israel were able to build up the temple to be God's habitation on earth and the city of Jerusalem to establish God's kingdom on earth.

C. Likewise, by enjoying the unsearchable riches of Christ, the believers in Christ are built up to be Christ's Body, the church, which is Christ's fullness, His expression (1:22-23), and which is also the habitation of God (2:21-22; 1 Tim. 3:15) and the kingdom of God (Matt. 16:18-19; Rom. 14:17).

D. Ultimately, God's habitation and God's kingdom will consummate in the New Jerusalem in eternity for the fulfillment of God's eternal economy; this miraculous structure of treasure is the goal of our enjoying and ministering the unsearchable riches of Christ as the treasure of the gospel (Rev. 21:1-3, 22; 22:1, 3).

WEEK 8 — DAY 1

Morning Nourishment

Eph. 3:8-11 To me, less than the least of all saints, was this grace given to announce to the Gentiles the unsearchable riches of Christ as the gospel and to enlighten all *that they may see* what the economy of the mystery is...in order that now...the multifarious wisdom of God might be made known through the church, according to the eternal purpose which He made in Christ Jesus our Lord.

In Ephesians 3 Paul told us that the revelation of the mystery concerning Christ for the church has been given to the apostles and prophets (v. 5). Paul's revelation of Christ was mainly a revelation of Christ's unsearchable riches....The apostle's preaching was focused on the riches of Christ, not on the doctrines. The riches of Christ are what Christ is to us, such as light, life, righteousness, and holiness. These riches are unsearchable; it is beyond our ability to trace them out. Since we also can be apostles and prophets, there is the need for us to see the unsearchable riches of Christ.

Paul...purposely indicated that the apostles and prophets were not extraordinary. On the contrary, they should be regarded simply as leading ones among the saints in the churches. They take the lead to receive the revelation concerning Christ for the church, to live Christ, to experience Christ, to enjoy Christ, and to minister the riches of Christ to others. If the enjoyment of the riches of Christ were available only for certain exceptional persons of high rank, then the rest of us would have no share in it. But in 3:8 Paul said that he was less than the least of all saints; yet he could preach the unsearchable riches of Christ as the gospel. The fact that Paul could do this indicates that we can do it also. Because he was less than we are, what was available to him is available also to us.

In order to be apostles, prophets, stewards, ministers, and even prisoners in Christ, we need to know the unsearchable riches of Christ. These riches are for the producing of the church to be the fullness of Christ. (*Life-study of Ephesians*, pp. 259-260)

WEEK 8 — DAY 1

Today's Reading

All the riches of Christ are for the producing of the church. This takes place through the divine dispensing of Christ into the believers. The church is produced not by teaching, nor by organizing, but by the dispensing of Christ. The more Christ is dispensed into us, the more life we have, the stronger life we have, the richer life we have, and the more uplifted the church life becomes. I love the ministry that dispenses the riches of Christ into the believers. By means of such a ministry, we have a proper, strong, uplifted church life.

The riches of Christ produce the church through the believers' experience and enjoyment of Christ. On Christ's side, it is a matter of dispensing, but on our side, it is a matter of experience and enjoyment. When we experience and enjoy the very Christ who is dispensed into us, we become part of the proper church life.

The riches of Christ also express God's multifarious wisdom (Eph. 3:10). God's wisdom is manifold; it has many aspects in many directions....The riches of Christ display His wisdom in a multifarious way. This is according to God's eternal purpose (v. 11).

The experience of the riches of Christ results in the fullness of Christ, the Body as Christ's expression (1:23)....Ephesians speaks both of the riches of Christ and of the fullness of Christ. A tall, husky man is the fullness of America because he has enjoyed the riches of American foodstuffs....[However, these] riches...did not make him this fullness until he ate them, digested them, and assimilated them....Likewise all the aspects of the riches of Christ do not become the fullness of Christ until they are eaten, enjoyed, digested, and assimilated by us. By absorbing these riches in such a way, we become the Body of Christ as His fullness to express Him. Thus, the Body of Christ is constituted of the riches of Christ that have been enjoyed and assimilated by us. Therefore, the Body is the result, the issue, of the experience and enjoyment of the riches of Christ. (*Life-study of Ephesians,* pp. 264-266)

Further Reading: Life-study of Ephesians, msg. 30

Enlightenment and inspiration:

Morning Nourishment

Isa. 40:25 To whom will you liken Me, that I should be compared? says the Holy One.

31 ...Those who wait on Jehovah will renew their strength; they will mount up with wings like eagles...

Num. 18:20 And Jehovah said to Aaron, You shall have no inheritance in their land, nor shall you have any portion among them; I am your portion and your inheritance among the children of Israel.

31 ...It is your reward in return for your service in the Tent of Meeting.

Our Savior, Jesus, is the Holy One, the eternal God, Jehovah, and the Creator of the heavens and the earth....As the Holy One, Jesus is unlimited, unsearchable, incomparable, and high (Isa. 40:12-14, 17-18, 28b, 22a). There is no comparison between Him and anyone or anything else. (Isa. 40:25, footnote 1)

To wait on the eternal God (v. 28) means that we terminate ourselves, i.e., that we stop ourselves with our living, our doing, and our activity, and receive God in Christ as our life, our person, and our replacement. Such a waiting one will be renewed and strengthened to such an extent that he will mount up with wings like eagles. He will not only walk and run but also soar in the heavens, far above every earthly frustration. This is...a regenerated and transformed person in the new creation.

In Isaiah 40 there are the announcing of the gospel (corresponding to the four Gospels—vv. 1-5), salvation through regeneration (corresponding to the Acts—Isaiah 40:6-8), and transformation (corresponding to the Epistles—vv. 28-31). (v. 31, footnote 1)

The eagles' wings signify the resurrection power of Christ, God's power in life, becoming our grace (cf. 1 Cor. 15:10; 2 Cor. 4:7; 12:9a). Those who stop themselves and wait on Jehovah will experience the power of resurrection, will be transformed, and will soar in the heavens (cf. Phil. 4:13; Col. 1:11). (footnote 2)

Today's Reading

Neither the priests nor the Levites (Num. 18:23b, 24b) had any inheritance or any portion in the land of Israel. God Himself was their portion and their inheritance among the sons of Israel (Deut. 10:9; 18:2; Josh. 13:33; Ezek. 44:28). Not only was God's food their portion—God Himself was their portion and their inheritance. Because God was their portion and inheritance, they did not need any other portion or inheritance. Cf. footnote 6 on Acts 26:18 and footnote 2 on Colossians 1:12. (Num. 18:20, footnote 1)

The reward, or compensation, given to Aaron and his sons as the priests (Num. 18:8-20) and to the serving Levites (vv. 21-32) altogether typifies Christ. In type, the priests and the Levites had no portion other than Christ. Christ was everything to them. Our service to God in the New Testament is not in the realm of material things; therefore, our reward is not in that realm. The only reward, the only compensation, for our priestly and Levitical service is Christ as everything to us (cf. Phil. 3:7-14). (v. 31, footnote 1)

[Romans 10:12-13 says, "There is no distinction between Jew and Greek, for the same Lord is Lord of all and rich to all who call upon Him; for 'whoever calls upon the name of the Lord shall be saved.'"] God selects us, redeems us, justifies us, sanctifies us, conforms us, and glorifies us in Christ in order that we may enjoy His unsearchable riches in Christ (Eph. 3:8). The secret to this enjoyment is to call on His name. (Rom. 10:12, footnote 1)

Calling on the name of the Lord is the secret not only to our salvation but also to our enjoyment of the Lord's riches. Beginning with Enosh, the third generation of mankind, and continuing all the way down to the New Testament believers, God's chosen and redeemed ones enjoyed Christ's redemption and salvation and all His riches by means of this secret (see footnote 1 on Acts 2:21). (v. 13, footnote 1)

To be saved here means to be brought into the enjoyment of the riches of the Lord. The Lord is rich to both Jews and Greeks. All who call on the Lord's name enjoy this rich Lord; as a result, they are filled with Him and express Him. (footnote 2)

Further Reading: Life-study of Ephesians, msg. 79

Enlightenment and inspiration: _____

_____

_____

Morning Nourishment

Eph. 3:2 If indeed you have heard of the stewardship of the grace of God which was given to me for you.

Eph. 3:17-19 ...That you...may be full of strength to apprehend with all the saints what the breadth and length and height and depth are and to know the knowledge-surpassing love of Christ, that you may be filled unto all the fullness of God.

In Ephesians 3 the apostle Paul had a very high vision.... [Here] he used the term "the unsearchable riches of Christ" (v. 8). What Paul saw regarding this is far beyond our understanding. Not even Paul himself had words adequate to express it. Eventually, he could speak only of "the breadth and length and height and depth" (v. 18). These dimensions, which are the dimensions of Christ, are actually the dimensions of the universe. As he was confined and restricted in a prison, Paul had a vision of the universal dimensions of Christ.

The stewardship of the grace is the dispensing of the riches of Christ. According to the context of chapter three, grace refers to the riches of Christ. When the riches of Christ are enjoyed by you, they become grace. Paul's ministry was to dispense the riches of Christ as grace to the believers....This is what we are doing in the ministry today.

This stewardship is according to God's economy. With God it is a matter of economy; with us it is a matter of stewardship. All the saints, no matter how insignificant they may seem to be, have a stewardship according to God's economy....Every saint can infuse Christ into others. Even a young sister in high school can dispense Christ into her classmates. This dispensing of Christ into others is the stewardship according to God's economy. (*Life-study of Ephesians,* pp. 244-245)

Today's Reading

Our concept of preaching the gospel needs to be uplifted. We should not be concerned merely with winning souls. Rather, we should preach the gospel to carry out God's economy by dispensing

God into others. Go to school or to work for the purpose of carrying out your stewardship according to God's economy for His dispensing. We are not doing an ordinary work of gospel preaching. We are dispensing God into man....We have the privilege of dispensing the unsearchable riches of Christ into others. (*Life-study of Ephesians,* p. 246)

[The unsearchable riches of Christ as the gospel are revealed in all twenty-seven books of the New Testament.] In the Gospels is the Christ who lived on the earth and died on the cross for the accomplishing of redemption. In the Acts is the resurrected and ascended Christ propagated and ministered to men. In Romans is the Christ who is our righteousness for justification and our life for sanctification, transformation, conformation, glorification, and building up. In Galatians is the Christ who enables us to live a life that is versus the law, religion, tradition, and forms. In Philippians is the Christ who is lived out of His members. In Ephesians and Colossians is the Christ who is the life, the content, and the Head of the Body, the church. In 1 and 2 Corinthians is the Christ who is everything in the practical church life. In 1 and 2 Thessalonians is the Christ who is our holiness for His coming back. In 1 and 2 Timothy and Titus is the Christ who is God's economy, enabling us to know how to conduct ourselves in the house of God. In the Epistles of Peter is the Christ who enables us to take God's governmental dealings administered through sufferings. In the Epistles of John is the Christ who is the life and fellowship of the children of God in God's family. In Revelation is the Christ who is walking among the churches in this age, ruling over the world in the kingdom in the coming age, and expressing God in full glory in the new heaven and new earth for eternity. In [Hebrews] is the present Christ, who is now in the heavens as our Minister (Heb. 8:2) and our High Priest (4:14-15; 7:26), ministering to us the heavenly life, grace, authority, and power and sustaining us to live a heavenly life on earth. (Heb. 1:3, footnote, 4)

Further Reading: Life-study of Ephesians, msg. 28

Enlightenment and inspiration: _____

WEEK 8 — DAY 4

Morning Nourishment

Deut. For Jehovah your God is bringing you to a good land,
8:7 a land of waterbrooks, of springs and of fountains, flowing forth in valleys and in mountains.

Col. Giving thanks to the Father, who has qualified you
1:12 for a share of the allotted portion of the saints in the light.

The good land, the land of Canaan, is a full, complete, and consummate type of the all-inclusive Christ, who is the embodiment of the Triune God (Col. 2:9) realized as the all-inclusive life-giving Spirit (1 Cor. 15:45; 2 Cor. 3:17), as the inheritance allotted to God's people for their enjoyment (Col. 1:12 and footnote 2; 2:6-7 and footnote 2 on v. 6; Gal. 3:14 and footnote 3). The riches of the good land in Deuteronomy 8:7-9 typify the unsearchable riches of Christ in different aspects (Eph. 3:8) as the bountiful supply to His believers in His Spirit (Phil. 1:19). The waterbrooks, springs, and fountains signify Christ as the flowing Spirit (John 4:14; 7:37-39; Rev. 22:1), and the valleys and mountains signify the different kinds of environments in which we may experience Christ as the flowing Spirit (cf. 2 Cor. 6:8-10). (Deut. 8:7, footnote 1)

Today's Reading

The land is good in its unsearchable riches. It is good in spaciousness, it is good in transcendency, and it is good in unsearchable riches.

First of all, it is rich in water....Deuteronomy says that the land is good in water. Listen to the different terms that are used: "a land of waterbrooks"—that means a land full of streams of waters—and a land "of springs and of fountains" (8:7)....With a well, there is always a spring. Underneath, at the bottom of the well, is a spring of water which feeds the well. The water issues from that spring and fills the well, and the well becomes the "fountain."...Then from this [fountain], there flows out a stream. You have the spring, then...the fountain, and then the stream.

These waters are types of the various kinds of supply of Christ's life. The life of Christ as the supply to us is just like the different kinds of waters. The Lord told us that out of the innermost part of those who believe on Him will flow rivers of living water.…This is the supply of the life of Christ as living water.… Many times you are thirsty—not thirsty in your physical body but thirsty in your spirit. When you come athirst to the Lord and contact Him,…you feel refreshed, you feel watered,…and your thirst is quenched.

Deuteronomy says that these waters are flowing forth from the valleys and the mountains.…Without valleys and mountains no water will be flowing. If all the land is a plain, there will be no flow of water. What are the valleys and the mountains?

In 2 Corinthians 6:8-10 Paul mentions many contrasting things, many mountains and valleys: "Through glory and dishonor, through evil report and good report; as deceivers and yet true; as unknown and yet well known; as dying and yet behold we live; as being disciplined and yet not being put to death; as made sorrowful yet always rejoicing; as poor yet enriching many; as having nothing and yet possessing all things."

"Glory" is a mountain; "dishonor" is a valley. The "evil report" is a valley; the "good report" is a mountain. "As sorrowful"—a valley; "yet always rejoicing"—a mountain. "As poor"—another valley; "yet enriching many"—not only a mountain but a great mountain. Some thought that Paul was a deceiver. But he was as a deceiver and yet true; with the valley there was a mountain. In these verses there are at least nine pairs, nine valleys and nine mountains. These are the places from which the water may flow.

[Deuteronomy 8:7 mentions] first the valleys, then the mountains.…The first place you contact the flowing water is in the valleys. Then if you trace that stream up to its origin, you find that it springs from the mountains. The stream is in the valley, but the spring is in the mountains. If you would have something flowing out from within you to water others, you must be in the valleys. (*The All-inclusive Christ,* pp. 39-40, 43-45)

Further Reading: The All-inclusive Christ, ch. 4

Enlightenment and inspiration: _____

Morning Nourishment

Deut. 8:8 A land of wheat and barley and vines and fig trees and pomegranates...

John 12:24 Truly, truly, I say to you, Unless the grain of wheat falls into the ground and dies, it abides alone; but if it dies, it bears much fruit.

[In Deuteronomy 8:8] wheat typifies the incarnated Christ, who was crucified and buried to multiply Himself (John 12:24), and barley, being the first-ripe grain (2 Sam. 21:9), points to the resurrected Christ as the firstfruits (1 Cor. 15:20). Vines typify the Christ who sacrificed Himself to produce wine to cheer God and man (Judg. 9:13; Matt. 9:17). The fig tree speaks of the sweetness and satisfaction of Christ as the life supply (Judg. 9:11); the pomegranates signify the fullness, the abundance and beauty, and the expression of the riches of Christ as life (Exo. 28:33-34; 1 Kings 7:18-20; S. S. 4:3b, 13); the bread signifies Christ as the bread of life (John 6:35, 48); the olive tree typifies Christ (Rom. 11:17) as the One who was filled with the Spirit and anointed with the Spirit (Luke 4:1, 18; Heb. 1:9); olive oil typifies the Holy Spirit, by whom we walk to honor God and whom we minister to honor man (Gal. 5:16, 25; 2 Cor. 3:6, 8; Judg. 9:9); and milk and honey (6:3) speak forth the goodness and sweetness of Christ (see note 2 on Exo. 3:8). (Deut. 8:7, footnote 1)

Today's Reading

[The Lord] put wheat first, not the barley or the vine [Deut. 8:8]. ...The wheat represents Christ incarnated. Christ is God incarnated as man to fall into the earth, to die and to be buried [John 12:24]. This is the wheat. It typifies the Christ who was incarnated, the Christ who died, and the Christ who was buried.

The barley points to...the resurrected Christ....In the land of Canaan, the barley always ripens first; among all the grains, the barley is first. In Leviticus 23:10 the Lord said: "Speak to the children of Israel, and say to them, When you come into the land which I am giving you, and reap its harvest, then you shall bring the sheaf of the firstfruits of your harvest to the priest." When the harvest

WEEK 8 — DAY 5

time came, the first fruits of the harvest must be offered to the Lord, and the first fruit was clearly the barley. Now we must read 1 Corinthians 15:20: "But now Christ has been raised from the dead, the firstfruits of those who have fallen asleep."...The first fruits of the harvest typify Christ as the firstfruits of resurrection.

Now let us see something concerning the trees. The first is a vine tree....In Judges 9:13 the vine said, "Shall I leave my new wine, which cheers God and men?" In one sense it depicts the sacrificing Christ, the Christ who has sacrificed everything of Himself. But this is not the main point. The main significance is that out of His sacrifice He produced something to cheer God and man—new wine.

The most happy person is the most unselfish one....We have no energy to sacrifice, for our life is a natural life, a selfish life. Only the life of Christ is a life of sacrifice. If you contact this Christ and experience His sacrificing life, He will energize you, He will strengthen you to sacrifice for God and for others. Then you will be the most happy person; you will be drunken with happiness. This is the experience of Christ as the vine tree.

Judges 9:11 tells us that the fig tree represents...the sweetness and satisfaction of Christ as our supply....Pomegranates...represent...the abundance and the beauty of life....When you enjoy and experience Christ as the wheat, as the barley, as the vine, and as the fig tree, the beauty of Christ is about you, and the abundance of the life of Christ is with you. This is the experience of Christ as the pomegranate. If you enjoy Christ as the resurrected One and by the power of His resurrection you live the life of Jesus on this earth to suffer all kinds of pressure, persecutions, troubles, and conflicts, you will realize the sweetness and satisfaction of Christ within you, and you will manifest the beauty and the abundance of life to others. When others touch you, they will sense the loveliness and attractiveness of Christ, and an abundance of life will be imparted to them. (*The All-inclusive Christ*, pp. 50-51, 57-59, 61, 63-64)

Further Reading: The All-inclusive Christ, chs. 5-6

Enlightenment and inspiration: _____

WEEK 8 — DAY 6

Morning Nourishment

Deut. 8:8-10 ...A land of olive trees with oil and of honey; a land in which you will eat bread without scarcity; you will not lack anything in it; a land whose stones are iron, and from whose mountains you can mine copper. And you shall eat and be satisfied, and you shall bless Jehovah your God for the good land which He has given you.

The olive tree...is the tree which produces olive oil....In Zechariah 4:12-14...there are two olive trees before the Lord, which...are the two sons of oil....Christ is the Son of oil; Christ is the man anointed with the Holy Spirit of God. God poured upon Him the oil of gladness. He is a man who is full of the Holy Spirit; He is the olive tree, the Son of oil....If we enjoy Him as the wheat, as the barley, as the vine, as the fig tree, and as the pomegranate, we will certainly enjoy Him as the olive tree;...we will be filled with the Spirit. We will be full of oil, and we will become an olive tree.

[Judges 9:9 says that olive oil] is used to honor God and honor man. If we would honor God or man, we must do it by the olive oil. This simply means that if we would serve the Lord, if we would help others, we must do it by the Holy Spirit. We must be a man filled with the Spirit, an olive tree, a son of oil....If we enjoy Him as the wheat, the barley, the vine, the fig tree, and the pomegranate, we will surely have the oil. We will be filled with the Holy Spirit. We will be truly able to honor God and others. (*The All-inclusive Christ*, p. 64)

Today's Reading

The good land is a land flowing with milk and honey....For the most part, honey has to do with the plant life...[but] without the bees we cannot have honey either....The greater part of milk belongs to the animal life. But indeed it is the product of both the animal life and the vegetable life....With both milk and honey, we enjoy the mingling of two kinds of life...the vegetable [the generating] and...the animal [the redeeming] lives.

[Christ] is a land flowing with milk and honey. This experience is produced from the two aspects of the life of Christ, the generating and the redeeming life. The more you realize Him as the wheat and the barley and so forth, and at the same time as the cattle and the flock, the more you will enjoy Christ as milk and honey.

We have seen three kinds of waters and at least eight kinds of food. Oh, how rich Christ is to us! We must have such an adequate and full experience of Him, not just as the living water, but as so many kinds of food. We must enjoy Christ to such an extent that the life within us may be matured. Then there will be a building for the Lord and the warfare with the enemy. (*The All-inclusive Christ,* pp. 68-69)

Stones signify Christ as material for building God's dwelling place (Isa. 28:16; Zech 4:7; 1 Pet. 2:4). The iron and copper are for making weapons (Gen. 4:22; 1 Sam. 17:5-7) and typify our spiritual warfare by which we fight the enemy (2 Cor. 10:4; Eph. 6:10-20). Iron also signifies Christ's ruling authority (Matt. 28:18; Rev. 19:15), and copper, Christ's judging power (Rev. 1:15 and footnote 1). The mountains from which copper is mined signify Christ's resurrection and ascension (Eph. 4:8 and footnote 1).

God's goal in His economy is not merely to redeem His people and save them from the world, typified by Egypt, but to bring them into Christ, typified by the good land, that they may possess Him and enjoy His unsearchable riches. By enjoying the riches of the land, the children of Israel were able to build up the temple to be God's habitation on earth and the city of Jerusalem to establish God's kingdom on earth. Likewise, by enjoying the unsearchable riches of Christ, the believers in Christ are built up to be Christ's Body, the church, which is Christ's fullness, His expression (Eph. 1:22-23), and which is also the habitation of God (Eph. 2:21-22; 1 Tim. 3:15) and the kingdom of God (Matt. 16:18-19; Rom. 14:17). Ultimately, God's habitation and God's kingdom will consummate in the New Jerusalem in eternity for the fulfillment of God's eternal economy (Rev. 21:1-3, 22; 22:1, 3). (Deut. 8:7, footnote 1)

Further Reading: Life-study of Ephesians, msgs. 81-82; *The All-inclusive Christ,* chs. 7-8

Enlightenment and inspiration: _____

WEEK 8 — HYMN

Hymns, #1164

1. Jesus, the all-inclusive land,
     Is everything to me:
   A Christ of brooks, of depths and streams,
     And fountains bubbling free.
   Springing from valleys and from hills,
   Flowing till every part He fills,
   He waters us—how glorious—
     By His life!

2. Jesus is now the land of wheat—
     Incarnate, crucified.
   But resurrection life is He
     By barley signified.
   He is a land of figs and vines—
   Blood of the grape, the cheering wine.
   With such supplies He satisfies—
     Christ our land!

3. O what a rich, abundant Christ:
     Our pomegranate true,
   The olive tree whose oil is now
     Anointing us anew.
   Rich milk and honey He doth bring,
   Sweet, satisfying, nourishing.
   Our Christ is such; He is so much!
     What a Christ!

4. In our good land we eat the bread—
     There is no scarcity.
   We never lack one thing in Him,
     So rich, so full is He.
   He is a land so vast, immense;
   He is complete in every sense.
   How He expands—land of all lands—
     In our heart!

5. Christ is a land of iron stones,
     Whence comes authority.
   We must dig out this solid Christ
     To bind His enemy.
   Then we must through the sufferings pass
   To be refined as burnished brass.
   With iron bind, as brass refined,
     Is our need.

WEEK 8 — PROPHECY

6 Lord, how we bless Thee for this land,
    The all-inclusive Christ!
   We've eaten Him, we're filled with Him,
    O how He has sufficed!
   Teach us to labor constantly
    Upon this vast reality;
   This is our joy, this our employ—
    Christ our land!

Composition for prophecy with main point and sub-points:

WEEK 9 — OUTLINE

The Mystery of the Gospel

Scripture Reading: Rom. 16:25; Eph. 1:9; 3:3-5, 9; 5:32; 6:19; Col. 1:26-27; 2:2; 4:3

Day 1

I. **The basic revelation in the Bible is the unveiling, the bringing to light, of God's mystery; for this reason, the Bible speaks of the revelation of the mystery (Rom. 16:25; Eph. 3:3, 5).**

II. **The gospel is the proclamation of Jesus Christ according to the revelation of the mystery; thus, Paul could speak of the mystery of the gospel (6:19).**

III. **There are five great mysteries in the Bible:**
   A. The mystery of the universe is God, who is the meaning and purpose of the universe (Gen. 1:1; Rev. 4:11; Eph. 3:9).
   B. The mystery of man is also God (Gen. 1:26; Zech. 12:1; 1 Cor. 2:11).
   C. The mystery of God is Christ (Col. 2:2).
   D. The mystery of Christ is the church (Eph. 3:4; Col. 4:3).
   E. The mystery of the church is the organism of Christ, the Body of Christ as the enlargement of Christ (Eph. 1:22-23; 4:4, 16; 5:30, 32).

Day 2

IV. **In Ephesians *mystery* is a crucial word:**
   A. In eternity God planned a will, but it was hidden in Him; hence, it was a mystery—the mystery of His will (1:9).
   B. God's hidden purpose is the mystery, and the unveiling of this mystery in the mingled spirit is the revelation of the mystery (3:3, 5).
   C. God's mystery is His hidden purpose, and with this mystery there is an economy—the economy of the mystery (v. 9).
   D. Christ is a mystery, and the church, as the Body of Christ to express Him, is the mystery of Christ (v. 4; Col. 4:3).
   E. Christ and the church as one spirit are the great mystery (1 Cor. 6:17; Eph. 5:32).

WEEK 9 — OUTLINE

Day 3

V. **The all-inclusive Christ, who indwells us, is the mystery of God's economy (Col. 1:26-27):**
   A. God's New Testament economy is like a great wheel, having Christ as its every part—He is the hub (the center), the spokes (the support), and the rim (the circumference) of the divine economy (Ezek. 1:15; Col. 1:17b, 18b):
      1. God's intention in His economy is to work Christ into His chosen people so that Christ may be all and in all (3:10-11; Gal. 1:16a; 2:20; 4:19).
      2. Christ is the mystery, the secret, the crucial focus, of the divine economy; this means that the secret of the dispensing of the Triune God into God's chosen people is Christ Himself (Col. 1:25-28, 17b, 18b; 2:9).
      3. Christ is the Head of the Body and the Body of the Head; He is all the members and in all the members of the new man (1 Cor. 12:12; Col. 1:18; 3:10-11).
   B. The mystery hidden from the ages and from the generations has been made manifest to the saints; this mystery is the all-inclusive Christ as the indwelling hope of glory (1:26-27):
      1. The hope of our calling is the hope of glory, which is the transfiguration of our body and the manifestation of the sons of God (Eph. 1:18b; 4:4b; Rom. 8:19, 23-25, 30; Phil. 3:21).
      2. The Christ who dwells within us is the mystery full of glory, with countless riches; we are being strengthened into our inner man according to the riches of God's glory, which are being wrought into us (Eph. 3:8, 14-17a).
      3. Christ as the mystery of God's economy is indwelling us as the hope of glory for our transformation from glory to glory unto the full expression of God (2 Cor. 3:18; Rev. 21:10-11).

Day 4

VI. **In particular, the mystery of the gospel is Christ and the church for the fulfillment of God's eternal purpose (Eph. 6:19):**

WEEK 9 — OUTLINE

A. The mystery of God is Christ, the Head (1:22; Col. 1:18):
  1. As the mystery of God, Christ is the history of God; the whole "story" of God is in Christ and is Christ (John 1:14; 1 Cor. 15:45b; Rev. 5:5).
  2. As the mystery of God, Christ is the definition, explanation, and expression of God—the Word of God (John 1:1; Rev. 19:13; Col. 2:2-3).
  3. As the mystery of God, Christ is the Firstborn of all creation (1:15).
  4. As the mystery of God, Christ is the Firstborn from the dead (v. 18).
  5. As the mystery of God, Christ is the embodiment of the Triune God (2:9).
  6. As the mystery of God, Christ is the life-giving Spirit dwelling in our spirit to be one spirit with us (1 Cor. 15:45b; 2 Tim. 4:22; 1 Cor. 6:17; Col. 3:4; Eph. 3:16-17a).
  7. As the mystery of God, Christ is the constituent of His Body, the church, which is the one new man (Col. 1:18; 3:10-11, 15).

Day 5
  8. As the mystery of God, Christ has the first place in all things (1:18b; 1 Cor. 2:2).

B. The mystery of Christ is the church, the Body of Christ (Eph. 3:4, 6, 10):
  1. Christ, the embodiment of God, is the expression of God, and the church, as the Body of Christ, is the expression of Christ (1:22-23).
  2. In God's economy mystery produces mystery: Christ, the mystery of God, brings forth the church, the mystery of Christ (Col. 2:2; 4:3).
  3. As the hidden mystery in God's eternal purpose, the church is a mystery within a mystery, for the church is the third stage of one mystery (Eph. 3:4, 9, 11):
    a. The first stage is God Himself as the mystery of the universe, the second stage is Christ as the mystery of God, and the third stage

WEEK 9 — OUTLINE

is the church as the mystery of Christ (John 1:18; Col. 2:2; 4:3).
  b. The church is the mystery of Christ, who is the mystery of God, who Himself is the mystery of the universe (Eph. 3:4, 9; Col. 2:2; Rev. 4:11).

Day 6
  4. The church is according to God's eternal purpose, and God created all things so that He could have the church (Eph. 3:9, 11; Rev. 4:11).
  5. The church is a constitution of the riches of Christ enjoyed and assimilated by the believers (Eph. 3:8).
  6. Through the church the multifarious wisdom of God is made known to the rulers and the authorities in the heavenlies (v. 10).
  7. Related to the mystery of Christ, the church, there is the economy of the mystery; God's economy is His plan and arrangement to dispense Himself in His Divine Trinity into His chosen people in order to produce the Body of Christ consummating in the New Jerusalem for the eternal corporate expression of the Triune God; this is the greatest mystery in the universe; nothing is greater or more important than this (v. 9; 1:22-23; 4:16; Rev. 21:2, 10-11).

VII. **All these mysteries are related to the gospel; thus, the mystery of the gospel refers to the entire New Testament economy, and through the gospel we may become persons of meaning and enjoy God as the mystery of the universe (Eph. 6:19; Psa. 36:8-9).**

WEEK 9 — DAY 1

> ## Morning Nourishment
>
> Rom. 16:25 Now to Him who is able to establish you according to my gospel, that is, the proclamation of Jesus Christ, according to the revelation of the mystery, which has been kept in silence in the times of the ages.
> Eph. 3:3 ...By revelation the mystery was made known to me...
> 6:19 And [praying] for me, that utterance may be given to me in the opening of my mouth, to make known in boldness the mystery of the gospel.
>
> In [Romans 16:25] we have a phrase that combines the mystery and the revelation. This phrase is *the revelation of the mystery*. In the New Testament the word *revelation* is used mainly with respect to the mystery of God. It does not refer to the ordinary things of human life.
>
> The Bible contains many doctrines, teachings, histories, and stories. All these things are related to the basic revelation either directly or indirectly.
>
> The basic revelation in the Bible is the unveiling of God's mystery. For this reason, the Bible speaks of the revelation of the mystery. The revelation of the mystery is the unveiling, the opening up, the bringing to light, of God's mystery so that we may see the central focus. This central focus is nothing less than Christ and His Body, the church. (*Basic Training*, pp. 27-28)

Today's Reading

The five great mysteries in the Bible are first, the mystery of the universe, which is God; second, the mystery of man, which is also God; third, the mystery of God, which is Christ; fourth, the mystery of Christ, which is the church; and fifth, the mystery of the church, which is the organism of Christ as the overflow and enlargement of Christ, the house of God, the golden lampstand, the bride, and the New Jerusalem. This is the ultimate mystery in the universe. Today, God is moving on in every place throughout the whole earth. Every local church is a mystery as the organism of Christ, the enlargement and overflow of Christ, the house of God, the golden lampstand, and the bride. Finally, in eternity we

WEEK 9 — DAY 1

will all become the ultimate expression of God—the New Jerusalem. Then God will achieve His ultimate goal in the universe. (*The Five Great Mysteries in the Bible*, p. 60)

[In Ephesians 6:19] Paul was asking the believers to pray that the word would be given to him. He desired to open his mouth with boldness to make known the mystery of the gospel. Paul needed both the word and the boldness to declare it.

The mystery of the gospel is Christ and the church for the fulfillment of God's eternal purpose. Some Christians preach a gospel in which there is no mystery. But Paul declared the mystery of the gospel. This mystery implies the entire New Testament economy. Christ is the mystery of God, and the church is the mystery of Christ. Both Christ and the church are for God's economy, which also is a mystery. All these mysteries are related to the gospel.

I believe that the Lord intends for a gospel preaching atmosphere to be developed in all the local churches. Pray for such an atmosphere to become prevailing. In our gospel meetings we must do more than sing and tell others that Christ can meet their need for satisfaction. On the contrary, we need to give full messages on the high things concerning God's economy. Let us tell the unbelievers of God's eternal intention. Do not underestimate their ability to understand. They may understand much more than you expect. Surely this kind of gospel preaching will draw unbelievers to the Lord.

In our gospel meetings we need to both preach and teach. We should teach in a preaching atmosphere. Surely the saints will want to bring their relatives and friends to this kind of meeting. Our burden is to make known the mystery of the gospel. Pray about this. Pray that the Lord will give us utterance and open our mouths with boldness to teach and to preach the mystery of the gospel. We all need to declare the gospel in this uplifted way. (*Life-study of Ephesians*, pp. 555-556)

Further Reading: Basic Training, msg. 2; The Five Great Mysteries in the Bible, chs. 1-2

Enlightenment and inspiration: _____
_____
_____
_____

WEEK 9 — DAY 2

Morning Nourishment

Eph. Making known to us the mystery of His will according
1:9 to His good pleasure, which He purposed in Himself.
3:4 By which, in reading *it*, you can perceive my understanding in the mystery of Christ.
5:32 This mystery is great, but I speak with regard to Christ and the church.

Besides the term *economy*, a number of other important terms are used by Paul in Ephesians. Three times in chapter one Paul mentions God's will: the good pleasure of His will (v. 5), the mystery of His will (v. 9), and the counsel of His will (v. 11). God has an economy because He has a will. In eternity God planned a will. This will was hidden in Him. Hence, it was a mystery. In His wisdom and prudence He has made this hidden mystery known to us through His revelation in Christ, that is, through Christ's incarnation, crucifixion, resurrection, and ascension. (*Life-study of Ephesians*, p. 630)

Today's Reading

In Ephesians the word *purpose* is used three times....In 1:11 Paul says that we have been predestinated according to the purpose of the One who operates all things according to the counsel of His will. In 3:11 Paul speaks of the eternal purpose,...[which is] the eternal plan of God made in eternity past. In 1:9 the word purpose is used as a verb: "Making known to us the mystery of His will according to His good pleasure, which He purposed in Himself." God has a purpose. Here the word *purpose* is the equivalent of the English word *plan*. God has a plan which He made in eternity. God has a plan because He has a will, a good pleasure, and an economy. According to His economy, He made a plan, a purpose.

Still another crucial word in Ephesians is *mystery*. As we have seen, 1:9 mentions the mystery of God's will. In 3:3 Paul says, "That by revelation the mystery was made known to me." God's hidden purpose is the mystery, and the unveiling of this mystery is revelation. In 3:4 Paul goes on to speak of the "mystery of Christ." The mystery of God in Colossians 2:2 is Christ, whereas the mystery of Christ here is the church. God is a mystery, and Christ, as the embodiment of God to express Him, is the mystery of God. Christ is also a mystery, and the church, as the Body of Christ to express Him, is the mystery of Christ.

In Ephesians 3:9 Paul speaks of enlightening all "that they may see what the economy of the mystery is." God's mystery is His hidden purpose. His purpose is to dispense Himself into His chosen people. Hence, there is an economy of the mystery of God. This mystery was hidden in God from the ages (that is, from eternity) and through all past ages, but now it has been brought to light to the New Testament believers. God's intention is to make known the dispensation, the economy, of His mystery.

Ephesians 5:32 and 6:19 also use the term *mystery*. In 5:32 Paul says, "This mystery is great, but I speak with regard to Christ and the church." The fact that Christ and the church are one spirit (1 Cor. 6:17), as typified by the husband and wife who are one flesh, is the great mystery. In 6:19 Paul speaks of making known in boldness the "mystery of the gospel." This mystery is Christ and the church for the fulfillment of God's eternal purpose.

It is important that we remember these crucial terms: *will, good pleasure, purpose, counsel, economy,* and *mystery*. On the one hand, these terms are deep and profound, and it would take years to understand them adequately. On the other hand, there is a simple secret to grasping their significance. This secret is Christ with the church. God's will is to have Christ with the church. Likewise, God's good pleasure and God's purpose are to have Christ with the church. We have already pointed out that Christ with the church is God's economy. Furthermore, God counseled with Himself to have Christ with the church. God's mystery is also related to Christ with the church. Therefore, Christ with the church is the secret to understanding these crucial terms. (*Life-study of Ephesians*, pp. 630-632)

Further Reading: Life-study of Ephesians, msg. 75; *The Five Great Mysteries in the Bible,* chs. 3-5

Enlightenment and inspiration:

WEEK 9 — DAY 3

Morning Nourishment

Col. 1:26-27 The mystery which has been hidden from the ages and from the generations but now has been manifested to His saints; to whom God willed to make known what are the riches of the glory of this mystery among the Gentiles, which is Christ in you, the hope of glory.

According to the picture presented in Ezekiel 1, God's New Testament economy is like a great wheel, having Christ as its every part....Christ is the hub, the center, of God's New Testament economy. Colossians 1:17 says that "all things cohere in Him," which means to exist together by Christ as the holding center, just as the spokes of a wheel hold together by the hub at their center....Christ is also the spokes, the support, of the great wheel of God's New Testament economy....Furthermore, He is the rim, the circumference. This means that God's entire New Testament economy and His move in His economy are just Christ. (*Messages to the Trainees in Fall 1990*, p. 142)

Today's Reading

What is of vital importance is that we see the vision of God's economy. God's economy is to work the living, all-inclusive person of Christ into us. According to the revelation in the book of Colossians, Christ is the portion of the saints, the Firstborn of all creation, the image of the invisible God, the Head of the Body, the Firstborn from among the dead, the One in whom all the fullness is pleased to dwell, the mystery of God's economy, the mystery of God, the reality of all positive things, and the constituent of the new man. Christ is everything: He is life, light, power, might, strength, righteousness, holiness, kindness, and every other divine attribute and human virtue. Because Christ is everything to us, He is all-inclusive. God's intention in His economy is to work this all-inclusive One into us.

Christ is the mystery, the secret, and the crucial focus of the divine economy. This means that the secret of the dispensing of the Triune God into God's chosen people is Christ Himself. Christ is the focal point of God's economy. God's economy is altogether related to Christ and focused on Him.

Although we were sinners, enemies, and rebels, ...we are sons of God, heirs of God, partners of Christ, and priests and kings. What a glory this is! If we see this glory, we shall also know the riches of the glory, even though we lack the language to utter these riches adequately. These riches include the divine life, the divine nature, the anointing, and the all-inclusive Spirit. Other aspects of the riches are righteousness, justification, holiness, sanctification, transformation, glorification, comfort, and the divine presence. It is impossible to list all the riches. They are beyond counting. These are the riches of the unique glory, the glory that is ours because we are sons and heirs of God, partners of Christ, and priests and kings.

All the blessings in the Bible are included in the riches of this glory, which is our portion. This glory is the glory of the mystery among the nations, and this mystery is Christ in us. The Christ who dwells within us is the mystery full of glory, with countless riches.

Because the Colossians had been distracted, Paul wrote to say that the mystery hidden from the ages and from the generations has been made manifest to the saints. This mystery is the all-inclusive Christ who indwells us. Because we have the One who is all in all, we have no need to turn to philosophies, ordinances, observances, and practices. How I look to the Lord that we all may be brought back to this mystery! Let us forget everything other than Christ and care only for Him.

It is crucial that we see the Christ who is the mystery hidden from eternity but now made manifest to the saints....God has willed to make known among the nations the riches of the glory of this mystery, which is Christ in us as the hope of glory. This mystery is the key to our Christian life and also to the church life. (*Life-study of Colossians,* pp. 330-331, 113, 116-118)

Further Reading: Life-study of Colossians, msgs. 14-15; *Life-study of Ephesians,* msg. 35; *The Conclusion of the New Testament,* msg. 180

Enlightenment and inspiration: _____

WEEK 9 — DAY 4

Morning Nourishment

Col. 2:2 That their hearts may be comforted, they being knit together in love and unto all the riches of the full assurance of understanding, unto the full knowledge of the mystery of God, Christ.

1:15 Who is the image of the invisible God, the Firstborn of all creation.

18 And He is the Head of the Body, the church; He is the beginning, the Firstborn from the dead, that He Himself might have the first place in all things.

The history of God is Christ. As the history of God, Christ is the mystery of God. Because the Jews do not have Christ, the God in whom they believe does not have such a history. Apart from Christ, there is neither the history of God nor the mystery of God.

As Christ is the history of God, so the church is the history of Christ. As the history of Christ, the church is the mystery of Christ. In the church we are a continuation of this history.

The Christ we have received is God with His wonderful history. As the all-inclusive One, Christ includes divinity, humanity, human living, crucifixion, resurrection, ascension, glorification, and enthronement. He includes all the divine attributes and human virtues. This is the One we have all received. (*Life-study of Colossians*, p. 421)

Today's Reading

The Word [John 1:1, 14] is the definition, explanation, and expression of God; hence, it is God defined, explained, and expressed. God is mysterious. He needs the Word to express Him. If you want to appear mysterious, the best way to do it is to be silent, for the more silent you are, the more mysterious you become. However, the more you talk, the more you expose yourself. All that is deep within you is revealed by your words. This is the meaning of the Word. Although God is a mystery, Christ as the Word of God defines, explains, and expresses Him. Thus, this Word is the definition, explanation, and expression of God. Eventually, this Word is God Himself, not God hidden, concealed, and mysterious, but

God defined, explained, and expressed. The Word is not the invisible God, but the very God who is visible. In the beginning this Word was with God; it was not separate from God, but always had God in Him. (*Life-study of John,* pp. 19-20)

Colossians 1:15...[says] that Christ is "the Firstborn of all creation." Christ is the first One among all creatures,...having the preeminence among all creatures. With regard to Christ being God, He is the Creator; but with regard to Christ being man, He is a creature. Since He became a man and partook of the created blood and flesh, to be sure He is part of creation. Among the creatures, after the first Adam fell, there was a last Adam....In God's creation, Christ is the first created One, who has preeminence in all creation.

In His resurrection, His physical body was transformed into a spiritual body....Through such a resurrection, He as the last Adam became the life-giving Spirit [1 Cor. 15:45]. Although He is the life-giving Spirit, He still has humanity.

Colossians 1:18 tells us that Christ is the Head of the Body, the church; He is the beginning, the Firstborn from the dead. This means that in resurrection Christ has the first place in the new creation, the church. He is the Head of the Body, the beginning, and the Firstborn from the dead, the first to be resurrected from the dead, to have the preeminence in the church. This shows us His relationship with the new creation.

Colossians 3:10-11 tells us that this all-inclusive Christ who is life within us makes us a corporate new man. This new man is composed of all the saints who have Him as life. The content of this new man is not our natural man: not Scythian nor Jew nor Chinese nor American nor German nor Japanese nor Filipino nor Malaysian. The content of this new man is Christ, who is the mystery of God and who is the life in all men. He is the life of the new man, and He is everything to the new man. (*The Five Great Mysteries in the Bible,* pp. 30-32, 37-38)

Further Reading: Life-study of Colossians, msgs. 18-19, 48; *The Mystery of God and the Mystery of Christ,* chs. 1-4

Enlightenment and inspiration:

WEEK 9 — DAY 5

Morning Nourishment

Eph. That in Christ Jesus the Gentiles are fellow heirs and
3:6 fellow members of the Body and fellow partakers of the promise through the gospel.
10-11 In order that now to the rulers and the authorities in the heavenlies the multifarious wisdom of God might be made known through the church, according to the eternal purpose which He made in Christ Jesus our Lord.

The mystery of God's economy is Christ. The Christ who indwells us is the mystery of this economy, an economy that involves God's administration of the whole universe. How profound! God has a universal economy, and the center, the focal point, of this economy is Christ. Furthermore, this economy is abstract, profound, and mysterious. The mystery of this universal economy, its indescribable element, is Christ....What need did [the Colossians] have for philosophy when they had the very Christ who is the mystery of God's universal economy? How vital it is for us to realize that the very Christ who is the mystery of God's economy dwells in us! (*Life-study of Colossians*, p. 124)

Today's Reading

The universe is a mystery, man is a mystery, and even more, God is a mystery. The Bible reveals these things very clearly, and there is no need for man to infer or grope. Then the Bible reveals another great mystery, which is the mystery of Christ. The mystery of Christ is the church. Colossians shows us that the mystery of God is Christ, while Ephesians shows us that the mystery of Christ is the church. These two books may be called sister books; one is on Christ and the other is on the church. All the "stories" of God are related to Christ, and all the "stories" of Christ are related to the church. The church came out of Christ; the church is also the expression of Christ. This is an exceedingly great mystery in the universe.

God is in Christ, and Christ is the embodiment of God....Today the church is the Body of Christ; Christ lives in this Body and is expressed through this Body. Hence, the church is a matter of Christ's life. The church has Christ as her life and everything. Just as God lived in Christ and was expressed through Christ, so Christ also lives in the church and is expressed through the church. The Head is Christ, and the Body is the church. The life of the Head is the life of the Body. All that the Head has is all that the Body has. In the Head there is God, and the Head is the expression of God; in the Body there is also God, and the Body is also the expression of God....In Christ we are not scattered; rather, we are one Body. There is nothing other than the Body that can express how intimate and inseparable our relationship is. This is an organic union. (*The Five Great Mysteries in the Bible,* pp. 45, 47)

When we consider Ephesians 3:4 in context, we see that the mystery of Christ is the church....God is a mystery, Christ is the mystery of God, and the church is the mystery of Christ. Hence, the church is actually a mystery within a mystery, for the church is a mystery in the third stage. The first stage is God Himself as the mystery of the universe; the second stage is Christ as the mystery of God; and the third stage is the church as the mystery of Christ.

As a mystery, the church is in the Triune God, in the Father, in the Son, and in the Spirit. With the believers there is an amount of mystery, but not as much as with the church. The divine mystery is much more with the church corporately than with the believers individually. The church is a corporate unit produced out of Christ, who is the mystery of God. This all-inclusive Christ is the mystery of the mysterious God, and such a Christ as the mystery of God produces a unit which is the church. By this we can realize that the church is the continuation of the mystery which is Christ. Mystery surely produces mystery. Christ, who is the mystery of God, brings forth the church, the mystery of Christ. (*The Conclusion of the New Testament,* pp. 2053-2055)

Further Reading: The Conclusion of the New Testament, msgs. 189-190; *The Mystery of God and the Mystery of Christ,* ch. 8

Enlightenment and inspiration: _____
_____
_____

WEEK 9 — DAY 6

Morning Nourishment

Eph. 3:8-9   To me, less than the least of all saints, was this grace given to announce to the Gentiles the unsearchable riches of Christ as the gospel and to enlighten all *that they may see* what the economy of the mystery is, which throughout the ages has been hidden in God, who created all things.

God's intention in His creation of all things, including man, was that man would be mingled with God to produce the church. Zechariah 12:1 says that the Lord stretched forth the heavens, laid the foundation of the earth, and formed the spirit of man within him. This indicates that the heavens are for the earth, that the earth is for man, and that man with the human spirit is for God. God's marvelous creation, focused on man, is for the purpose of producing the church. Therefore, Ephesians 3:9 speaks of the mystery hidden in God, who created all things.

According to Ephesians 1:5 and 9, the motive of God's creating of all things was His desire and pleasure.

The basis of God's work in creation was God's will and plan (Eph. 1:10-11). Revelation 4:11 says that all things were created according to God's will. God is a God of purpose, having a will of His own pleasure. He created all things for His will that He might accomplish and fulfill His purpose. God has a will, and according to that will He conceived His plan. Then according to that will and plan, He created all things so that He may have the church. (*The Conclusion of the New Testament*, pp. 2055-2056)

Today's Reading

It is through the church as the mystery of Christ that God's multifarious wisdom will be made known to the rulers and authorities in the heavenlies. Ephesians 3:10 says, "In order that now to the rulers and the authorities in the heavenlies the multifarious wisdom of God might be made known through the church." The church is produced from the unsearchable riches of Christ, as revealed in 3:8. When God's chosen people partake of and enjoy the riches of Christ, these riches constitute them the church, through which God's multifarious wisdom is made known to the angelic rulers and authorities in the heavenlies. Hence, the church is God's wise exhibition of all that Christ is. (*The Conclusion of the New Testament,* p. 2062)

The economy of the mystery in Ephesians 3:9 is the dispensing of the unsearchable riches of Christ in verse 8. When we preach the gospel, we bring the Head into sinners. When we edify the saints, we bring more and more of the Head into the Body. Whatever we do today must be for the dispensing of Christ as the Head into all His members. Then, at the fullness of times, at least a part of the Body will be ready, mature, and ripe—good for being taken up. This will be the rapture, the day of the wedding of the Lamb. Now we are not only waiting for that day, we are passing through a process under the dispensing of Christ. This is God's economy. God's desire is that all men see what the economy of the mystery is (3:9). Now we are under the dispensing of Christ. God is daily and hourly dispensing all the unsearchable riches of Christ into us. (*Enjoying the Riches of Christ for the Building Up of the Church as the Body of Christ,* pp. 19, 23)

The Son of God is the embodiment of God. God's economy is to dispense Himself into a great number of human beings in order to produce a Body for this embodiment of Himself. This means that the Son of God as the embodiment of God requires a Body, an increase, an expansion. This expansion can be produced only by God's dispensing of Himself into His chosen people. This is the greatest mystery in the universe. (*Life-study of Ephesians,* p. 250)

Without God, the entire universe is empty and dead. The meaning of the universe is the living God. As the living Spirit, He is omnipresent....You need only to open your heart and pray to Him, and He will enter into you. Then you will become a person with meaning, and you will enjoy God as the mystery of the entire universe. (*The Five Great Mysteries in the Bible,* pp. 17-18)

Further Reading: Life-study of Ephesians, msgs. 7, 29, 31; The Mystery of the Universe and the Meaning of Human Life, chs. 1-2

Enlightenment and inspiration: _____
_____
_____

WEEK 9 — HYMN

Hymns, #818

1. Christ is the mystery of God;
   God is invisible, unshown,
   His image man hath never seen,
   But Christ the Son hath made Him known.

2. Christ is the very Word of God,
   He is God's explanation true;
   God's full embodiment is He
   And God's own image brings to view.

3. Image of God invisible,
   Effulgence of God's glory fair;
   God's fulness ever dwells in Him,
   God's testimony He doth bear.

4. The Church the myst'ry is of Christ,
   For He is now to man unshown;
   No man on earth may see Him now,
   But thru the Church He is made known.

5. The Church is Christ's expression full,
   In her Christ dwelleth bodily;
   She is His duplication true,
   And man in her Himself may see.

6. The Church the image has of Christ,
   She is His increase and His spread;
   Christ's very self is found in her,
   The Body, she, to Christ the Head.

7. Thus, in the Son the Father is,
   And now the Spirit is the Son;
   The Spirit of the Triune God
   Is in the Church and with her one.

WEEK 9 — PROPHECY

Composition for prophecy with main point and sub-points: _____

WEEK 10 — OUTLINE

Serving God in Our Spirit in the Gospel of His Son

Scripture Reading: Rom. 1:1, 9; 15:16

Day 1
I. For all the requirements related to the believers revealed in the New Testament, especially that of announcing the gospel of God, we need to receive the divine supply of the Body through the dispensing of the processed Triune God (Eph. 3:2; Heb. 4:16; Rom. 5:17, 21; John 7:37-38; Acts 6:4; Phil. 1:5-6, 19-25).

II. We need to see that our service to God in the gospel is our worship to God; in the New Testament, serving God is actually the same as worshipping God (Matt. 4:9-10; S. S. 1:2; cf. Psa. 2:11-12):

A. Paul said that the believers at Thessalonica "turned to God from the idols to serve a living and true God" (1 Thes. 1:9):

1. God must be living to us and in us in every aspect of our daily life; the fact that God controls, directs, corrects, and adjusts us, even in such small things as our thoughts and motives, is a proof that He is living (Phil. 1:8; 2:5, 13; 1:20).

2. We live under the control, direction, and correction of a living God to be a pattern of the glad tidings that we spread (1 Thes. 1:5-8; 2:10; 2 Thes. 3:5).

B. As believers in Christ, we must live a life in our spirit which bears the testimony that the God whom we worship and serve is living in the details of our life; the reason we do not do or say certain things should be that God is living in us (Rom. 8:6, 16).

Day 2
III. Paul said that he was "separated unto the gospel of God" (1:1), and he declared, "God is my witness, whom I serve in my spirit in the gospel of His Son" (v. 9):

WEEK 10 — OUTLINE

A. The Greek word for *serve* in Romans 1:9 means "serve in worship," as used in Matthew 4:10, 2 Timothy 1:3, Philippians 3:3, and Luke 2:37; Paul considered his preaching of the gospel as a worship and service to God, not merely a work.

B. When we come to serve God, or worship God, we need a blood-purified conscience; our defiled conscience needs to be purified so that we may serve God in a living way (Heb. 9:14; 10:22; 1 John 1:7, 9; Acts 24:16; cf. 1 Tim. 4:7).

C. To serve God in the gospel is to serve Him in the all-inclusive Christ, because the gospel is simply Christ Himself (Acts 5:42; Rom. 1:3-4; 8:29).

D. In order to preach the gospel of God's Son, we must be in our regenerated spirit (1:9); in the book of Romans Paul stressed that whatever we are (2:29; 8:5-6, 9), whatever we have (vv. 10, 16), and whatever we do toward God (1:9; 7:6; 8:4, 13; 12:11) must be in our spirit.

E. Paul served God in his regenerated spirit by the indwelling Christ, the life-giving Spirit, not in his soul by the power and ability of the soul; this is the first important item in his preaching of the gospel.

Day 3

F. The gospel of God, unto which Paul was separated, is the subject of the book of Romans; the book of Romans may be regarded as the fifth gospel (1:1; 2:16; 16:25):

 1. The first four Gospels are concerning the incarnated Christ, Christ in the flesh, living among His disciples; the gospel in Romans is concerning the resurrected Christ as the Spirit living within His disciples (8:2, 6, 9-11, 16).

 2. We need the fifth gospel, the book of Romans, to reveal the subjective Savior within us as the subjective gospel of Christ.

 3. The central message of the book of Romans is that God desires to transform sinners in the flesh into sons of God in the spirit in order to

constitute the Body of Christ expressed as the local churches (v. 29; 12:1-5; ch. 16).
   4. All of us need to function as priests of the gospel of God according to the revelation of the book of Romans; we need to learn the elements and details of the gospel, we need to experience the full content of the gospel, and we need to exercise our spirit to learn how to minister the gospel (15:16).

Day 4 IV. **"God is Spirit, and those who worship Him must worship in spirit and truthfulness" (John 4:24):**
   A. To contact God the Spirit with the spirit is to drink of the living water, and to drink of the living water is to render real worship to God (vv. 10-14).
   B. God so loved the world that He gave His only begotten Son for sinners to believe into Him and drink of Him as the flowing Triune God in order for them to become the totality of eternal life, the New Jerusalem (3:16; 4:14b; cf. Jer. 2:13).
   C. According to typology, God should be worshipped in the place chosen by Him for His habitation (Deut. 12:5, 11, 13-14, 18) and with the offerings (Lev. 1—6); the place chosen by God for His habitation typifies the human spirit (Eph. 2:22), and the offerings typify Christ (Heb. 10:5-10).
   D. The divine reality is Christ as the reality of all the offerings of the Old Testament for the worship of God (John 14:6; 1:29; 3:14) and as the fountain of living water, the life-giving Spirit (4:7-15), partaken of and drunk by His believers to become the reality within them (1 Cor. 12:13; John 7:37-39).
   E. By enjoying Christ as the divine reality of the offerings in our spirit, He becomes our genuineness and sincerity (truthfulness) for the true worship of God (4:24).

V. **"We are the circumcision, the ones who serve by the Spirit of God and boast in Christ Jesus**

WEEK 10 — OUTLINE

and have no confidence in the flesh" (Phil. 3:3; cf. Rom. 2:28-29):

A. The flesh refers to all that we are and have in our natural being; anything natural, whether it is good or evil, is the flesh (Phil. 3:4-6).

B. As believers in Christ, we should not trust in anything that we have by our natural birth, for everything of our natural birth is part of the flesh.

C. Even though we have been regenerated, we may continue to live in our fallen nature, boast in what we do in the flesh, and have confidence in our natural qualifications; therefore, it is important that we be deeply and personally touched by these verses in Philippians 3.

D. We need the Lord's light to shine on us concerning our nature, our deeds, and our confidence in the flesh; we need to be enlightened by the Lord to see that we still live too much by the flesh and that we boast in our deeds and qualifications.

E. One day, when the light shines on us concerning this, we will want to prostrate ourselves before the Lord and confess how unclean our nature is; then we will condemn everything we do by our fallen nature; we will see that in the eyes of God whatever is done in the fallen nature is evil and worthy of condemnation.

F. Formerly, we boasted in our deeds and qualifications, but the time will come when we will condemn the flesh with its qualifications; then we shall boast in Christ alone, realizing that in ourselves we have absolutely no ground for boasting.

G. Only when we have been enlightened by God shall we be able to say truly that we have no trust in our natural qualifications, ability, or intelligence; only then shall we be able to testify that our confidence is wholly in the Lord; after we are enlightened in this way, we shall truly serve and worship God in our spirit and by the Spirit.

Day 5 VI. **In order to serve God in the gospel of His Son,** we need to see that we are men in the flesh, worthy of nothing but death and burial—this is to follow the Lord's pattern to fulfill all righteousness and enter into the ministry of the age (Matt. 3:13-17; 21:32):

A. The base for Jesus to be baptized is that He considered Himself, according to His humanity, a man, especially an Israelite, who is a man "in the flesh" (John 1:14); even though He was only "in the likeness of the flesh of sin" (Rom. 8:3), "without sin" (Heb. 4:15), yet He was "in the flesh," which has nothing good but is worthy only of death and burial.

B. Based upon this fact, at the beginning of His ministry for God, He was willing to be baptized by John the Baptist, recognizing that, according to His humanity, He was one who did not have any qualification to be a servant of God.

C. As a man in the flesh, He needed to be a dead man buried in the death water to fulfill God's New Testament requirement according to His righteousness, and He did it willingly, considering it the fulfilling of God's righteousness.

D. This shows that we should not bring anything of our natural life, anything of our flesh, into God's ministry in the service of His gospel.

E. We all should declare in our life and work, "I am a person in the flesh, worthy of nothing but death and burial, so I want to have myself terminated, crucified, and buried" (Gal. 2:20).

VII. **Our work and labor for the Lord in the gospel is not by our natural life and natural ability but by the Lord's resurrection life and power; resurrection is the eternal principle in our service to God (Num. 17:8; 1 Cor. 15:10, 58; 16:10):**

A. The life-giving Spirit is the reality of the Triune God, the reality of resurrection, and the reality of the Body of Christ (John 16:13-15; 20:22; 1 Cor. 15:45b; Eph. 4:4).

Day 6

B. Resurrection means that everything is of God and not of us, that God alone is able and that we are not able, and that everything is done by God and not by ourselves (Num. 17:8).
C. All those who know resurrection have given up hope in themselves; they know that they cannot make it; everything that is of death belongs to us, and everything that is of life belongs to the Lord (2 Cor. 1:8-9; cf. Eccl. 9:4).
D. We must acknowledge that we are nothing, have nothing, and can do nothing; we must come to the end of ourselves to be convinced of our utter uselessness (Exo. 2:14-15; 3:14-15; Luke 22:32-34; 1 Pet. 5:5-6).
E. The resurrected Christ as the life-giving Spirit lives in us, enabling us to do what we could never do in ourselves (1 Cor. 15:10; 2 Cor. 1:8-9, 12; 4:7-18).
F. When we do not live by our natural life but live by the divine life within us, we are in resurrection; the issue of this is the reality of the Body of Christ as the goal of the gospel of God (Phil. 3:10-11; Eph. 1:22-23).

WEEK 10 — DAY 1

Morning Nourishment

Eph. If indeed you have heard of the stewardship of the
3:2 grace of God which was given to me for you.

1 Thes. For they themselves report concerning us what kind
1:9 of entrance we had toward you and how you turned to God from the idols to serve a living and true God.

The believers experience the divine dispensing of the Divine Trinity in various other aspects, including serving and worshipping God, working and laboring for the Lord, not loving the world, overcoming Satan, fighting the good fight, running the course of the race, being profited by all things in their circumstances and environments, having the best attitude toward others, and watching and praying. For all of these matters we surely need the dispensing of the Divine Trinity. However, few Christians realize this. We need to see that in order to carry out these matters, we need God's divine supply, which comes to us through His divine dispensing.

Without [the divine dispensing of the processed Triune God] we cannot receive the supply, and without this supply we cannot fulfill the requirements mentioned in the New Testament. If we would meet what the New Testament requires of the believers, we need the divine supply, even the very essence of the Triune God. (*The Conclusion of the New Testament*, pp. 1827-1828)

Today's Reading

In ourselves we cannot meet any of the divine requirements. For example, we cannot fulfill the requirement to worship God. Some may think that to worship God is easy and natural. Actually, no one can truly worship God without God's dispensing of His element into him. We cannot render to God the worship that satisfies Him, that is accepted by Him as a real pleasure to Him, apart from the dispensing of the divine essence into our being. But through this divine dispensing we can worship God in a way that satisfies Him.

It is altogether necessary for us to contact the processed Triune God that we may receive His supply through His dispensing of Himself into our being. We need to be reminded repeatedly of our need for the dispensing of the processed Triune God.

WEEK 10 — DAY 1

In the New Testament serving God is actually the same thing as worshipping God. You cannot serve God without worshipping Him. Neither can you worship Him without serving Him. For instance, in Matthew 4 the Lord Jesus was tempted by the devil concerning worship. Referring to the kingdoms of the world and their glory, the devil said to Him, "All these will I give You if You will fall down and worship me" (v. 9). The Lord Jesus answered, "It is written, You shall worship the Lord your God, and Him only shall you serve" (v. 10). Here we see that to worship actually means to serve. Hence, to worship God is to serve God. Without serving God we cannot render real worship to Him.

In 1 Thessalonians 1:9b Paul says that the believers at Thessalonica "turned to God from the idols to serve a living and true God." Literally, the Greek word rendered "serve" here means to serve as a slave. As used in verse 9, the word serve is all-inclusive. It includes everything we do in our daily living.

By our daily life we prove that God is living. If God were not living, our daily life would be very different from what it is. Our present living is a testimony that the God whom we serve is living. He is living in us, and He controls us, directs us, and deals with us. He will not let us go. Rather, in many matters He corrects us and adjusts us. The fact that God controls us and directs us, even in such small things as our thoughts and motives, is a proof that He is living. We live under the control, direction, and correction of a living God. As believers in Christ we must live a life which bears the testimony that the God we worship and serve is living in the details of our life. The proper Christian life should bear a testimony that God is living. The reason we do not do or say certain things should be that God is living in us. The God whom we worship and serve is living not only in the heavens but also in us. We have turned to God from idols to serve a living and true God. No doubt, when God is living to us in our experience, He is also true. (*The Conclusion of the New Testament,* pp. 1828-1830)

Further Reading: The Conclusion of the New Testament, msg. 168

Enlightenment and inspiration: _____

WEEK 10 — DAY 2

Morning Nourishment

Rom. Paul, a slave of Christ Jesus, a called apostle, sepa-
1:1 rated unto the gospel of God.
9 For God is my witness, whom I serve in my spirit in
the gospel of His Son...
2 Tim. I thank God, whom I serve from *my* forefathers in a
1:3 pure conscience...

When we come to serve God, or worship God, we need to have a pure conscience, a conscience purified from dead works or from any kind of offense. Hebrews 9:14 says, "How much more will the blood of Christ, who through the eternal Spirit offered Himself without blemish to God, purify our conscience from dead works to serve the living God?" On the cross, Christ offered Himself to God in a human body, which is a matter of time. But He offered Himself through the eternal Spirit, who is of eternity, without any limit of time. Because Christ offered Himself by the eternal Spirit, His blood has an eternal efficacy to purify our conscience so that we may serve and worship the living God.

To serve the living God requires a blood-purified conscience. To worship in dead religion...does not require our conscience to be purified. The conscience is the leading part of our spirit. The living God, whom we desire to serve, always comes to our spirit (John 4:24) by touching our conscience. He is righteous, holy, and living. Our defiled conscience needs to be purified so that we may serve Him in a living way. To worship God in our mind religiously does not require this. (*The Conclusion of the New Testament*, p. 1830)

Today's Reading

Hebrews 9:14 speaks of "dead works" and "the living God." Because we were dead (Eph. 2:1; Col. 2:13), whatever we did, bad or good, was dead works in the sight of the living God. The book of Hebrews does not teach religion; it reveals the living God (3:12; 9:14; 10:31; 12:22). To touch this living God we need to exercise our spirit and to have a blood-purified conscience. The blood of Christ was shed for the forgiveness of sins (Matt. 26:28), and the new covenant was consummated with it (Heb. 10:29; Luke 22:20).

It has accomplished eternal redemption for us (Heb. 9:12; Eph. 1:7; 1 Pet. 1:18-19), and now it washes us from our sins (Rev. 1:5; 1 John 1:7) and purifies our conscience so that we may serve and worship the living God. The believers serve and worship God in their spirit in the gospel of God's Son. Paul says, "God is my witness, whom I serve in my spirit in the gospel of His Son" (Rom. 1:9a). The Greek word translated "serve" here means to serve in worship of God.

If we would serve God and worship Him, we must do this in our spirit for the preaching of the gospel. The New Testament service and worship are carried out in the preaching of the gospel. This gospel is not concerned with anything other than God's Son. The gospel of God's Son refers to the all-inclusive Christ. Therefore, to serve God in the gospel is to serve Him in the all-inclusive Christ. In the New Testament the gospel is simply Christ Himself. This is the reason Acts 5:42 says that the apostles were "announcing the gospel of Jesus as the Christ."

In Romans 1:9a Paul said that he served God in his spirit. This indicates that in order to preach the gospel of God's Son, we must be in our spirit. Preaching the gospel depends on our spirit. Whenever we preach the gospel, we should exercise our spirit.

Only in the book of Romans does Paul say that he serves God in his spirit. The reason is that in Romans Paul is arguing with religious people who invariably are in something other than the spirit—in letters, forms, or doctrines. In Romans Paul indicates that whatever we do toward God must be done in our spirit, that whatever we are must be in spirit, and that whatever we have must be in spirit. In 2:29 he says that the genuine people of God must be in spirit, that true circumcision is not outward in the flesh but in the spirit. Then in 7:6 he says that we should serve God in newness of spirit. Finally, in 12:11 Paul says that we must be burning in spirit. Preaching the gospel of God is absolutely a matter of our spirit. (*The Conclusion of the New Testament,* pp. 1830-1832)

Further Reading: The Conclusion of the New Testament, msg. 168

Enlightenment and inspiration: _____

Morning Nourishment

Rom. ...The gospel of God, which He promised beforehand
1:1-3 through His prophets in the holy Scriptures, concerning His Son...

15:16 That I might be a minister of Christ Jesus to the Gentiles, a laboring priest of the gospel of God, in order that the offering of the Gentiles might be acceptable, having been sanctified in the Holy Spirit.

The gospel of God in which we serve God in our spirit is actually the subject of the book of Romans. In the very first verse of this book Paul says that as a slave of Christ and a called apostle he was "separated unto the gospel of God." This indicates that Paul's intention in Romans is to write concerning the gospel. The entire book unfolds the gospel, the glad tidings of God, in its fullest way.

Paul refers to his Epistle to the Romans as a gospel. In 2:16 he says, "When God judges the secrets of men according to my gospel through Jesus Christ." Paul also believed that God would establish the saints according to his gospel: "Now to Him who is able to establish you according to my gospel, that is, the proclamation of Jesus Christ" (16:25). Therefore, the book of Romans may be regarded as the fifth gospel. (*The Conclusion of the New Testament*, p. 1832)

Today's Reading

The gospel in the first four books of the New Testament—Matthew, Mark, Luke, and John—concerns Christ in the flesh as He lived among His disciples before His death and resurrection. The gospel in Romans concerns Christ as the Spirit, not Christ in the flesh. In Romans 8 we see that the Spirit of life who indwells us is simply Christ Himself....The Christ in the four Gospels was among the disciples; the Christ in Romans is within us....This Christ is deeper and more subjective than the Christ in the four Gospels.

If we have only the gospel concerning Christ as revealed in the first four books of the New Testament, our gospel is too objective. We need the fifth gospel, the book of Romans, to reveal the subjective gospel of Christ. Our Christ is not merely the Christ in the flesh after incarnation and before resurrection, the Christ who was among His disciples. Our Christ is deeper and more subjective. He is the Spirit of life within us. Although John 14 and 15 reveal that Christ will be in His disciples, that was not fulfilled before His resurrection....Romans is the gospel of Christ after His resurrection, revealing that He is now the subjective Savior in His believers. Therefore, this gospel is deeper and more subjective.

The central message of the book of Romans is that sinful, fleshly people can be made sons of God and conformed to the image of the Son of God. In this way Christ becomes the Firstborn among many brothers (8:29). Thus, the central point of the gospel is not forgiveness of sins. It is the producing of the sons of God, many brothers of the Son of God. God desires to transform sinners in the flesh into sons of God in the spirit. If we would serve God in the gospel, we all should make this same matter our goal. We preach the gospel not simply that people may be saved or be forgiven of their sins or become spiritual, but that they may become sons of God. This is our aim....For Paul, the preaching of the gospel, the serving of God in the gospel of His Son, was a priestly ministry, a priestly service [15:16]. As believers, we all should serve God in such a priestly way in the gospel of His Son.

Whenever we contact anyone, whether a believer or an unbeliever, we need to know his need as far as the gospel is concerned. If a person is not clear about salvation, we should help him to be clear and even joyful in God's salvation. We need to serve him with the gospel. Others may be clear about salvation but not about other aspects of the gospel. Thus, we must minister something to meet their needs.

The crucial point in serving God in our spirit in the gospel of His Son is that we minister Christ to others in the gospel. For this, we need to learn the elements and details of the gospel, we need to experience the full content of the gospel, and we need to exercise our spirit. This is to serve God in our spirit in the gospel of God's Son. (*The Conclusion of the New Testament,* pp. 1832-1834)

Further Reading: *The Advance of the Lord's Recovery Today,* ch. 1

Enlightenment and inspiration: _____

Morning Nourishment

John 4:23-24 But an hour is coming, and it is now, when the true worshippers will worship the Father in spirit and truthfulness, for the Father also seeks such to worship Him. God is Spirit, and those who worship Him must worship in spirit and truthfulness.

Phil. 3:3 For we are the circumcision, the ones who serve by the Spirit of God and boast in Christ Jesus and have no confidence in the flesh.

The believers not only serve God in their spirit but also serve Him by the Spirit of God...(Phil. 3:3a)....*Serve* means to serve as priests. All New Testament believers are priests to God (1 Pet. 2:9; Rev. 1:6)....As priests, we must serve God and worship Him in our spirit and by His Spirit.

The believers serve and worship God in spirit and truthfulness...(John 4:23-24). In typology the worship of God should be in the place chosen by God to set His habitation there (Deut. 12:5, 11, 13-14, 18) and with the offerings (Lev. 1—6). The place chosen by God for His habitation typifies the human spirit, where God's habitation is today (Eph. 2:22). The offerings typify Christ. Christ is the fulfillment and reality of all the offerings with which God's people in the Old Testament worshipped Him. Hence,...we should contact God the Spirit in our spirit, instead of in a specific place, and through Christ, instead of with the offerings, for now, because Christ the reality has come, all the shadows and types are over. God is Spirit, and to worship God is to contact Him....Today we worship God in our spirit with Christ as the reality of all the offerings. (*The Conclusion of the New Testament*, pp. 1834-1836)

Today's Reading

In serving and worshipping God the believers should have no confidence in their flesh...(Phil. 3:3b)....We may think that to trust in the flesh simply means to trust in the fallen human nature. But this is actually not the meaning of "flesh" in Philippians 3:3b. After saying that we should not have any confidence in the flesh, Paul goes on to say that he was circumcised on the eighth day, that he was of the race of Israel, that he was of the tribe of Benjamin, that he was a Hebrew of the Hebrews, that according to the law he was a Pharisee, that according to zeal he persecuted the church, and that according to the righteousness of the law he was blameless. All these things were aspects of Paul's flesh. However, we may think that the flesh includes only evil things but not good things. Nevertheless, the honorable, lovable, and superior aspects of our natural being are still the flesh....Anything natural, whether it is good or evil, is the flesh....As believers in Christ we should not trust in anything we have by our natural birth, for everything of our natural birth is part of the flesh. In order to render genuine service and worship to God, everything we do must be by the Spirit of God, in Christ, and with no trust in the flesh.

Even though we have been regenerated, we may continue to live in our fallen nature, boast in what we do in the flesh, and have confidence in our natural qualifications....We need the Lord's light to shine on us concerning our nature, our deeds, and our confidence in the flesh....Although we have been regenerated to become children of God with the divine life and nature, we still live too much in the flesh. One day, when the light shines on you concerning this, you will want to prostrate yourself before the Lord and confess how unclean your nature is. Then you will condemn everything you do by your fallen nature....Formerly, we boasted in our deeds and qualifications. But the time will come when...we shall condemn [the flesh]. Then we shall boast in Christ alone, realizing that in ourselves we have absolutely no ground for boasting.

Only when we have been enlightened by God shall we be able to say truly that we have no trust in our natural qualifications, ability, or intelligence. Only then shall we be able to testify that our confidence is wholly in the Lord. After we are enlightened in this way, we shall truly serve and worship God in our spirit and by the Spirit. (*The Conclusion of the New Testament*, pp. 1836-1838)

Further Reading: A Word of Love to the Co-workers, Elders, Lovers, and Seekers of the Lord, ch. 2; Basic Lessons on Service, lsn. 16

Enlightenment and inspiration: _____

Morning Nourishment

Matt. **...Jesus came...to John to be baptized by him. But
3:13-15 John tried to prevent Him, saying,** *It is I who* **have
need of being baptized by You....But Jesus answered
and said to him, Permit it for now, for it is fitting for us
in this way to fulfill all righteousness....**

21:32 **For John came to you in the way of righteousness, and
you did not believe him, but the tax collectors and the
harlots believed him....**

When the people received John [the Baptist]'s preaching and came to repent to him, he right away baptized them by putting them into the water to bury them, indicating that they were men of the flesh who had nothing good (Rom. 7:18) and were worthy only of death and burial. Perhaps some people thought that there should be a good result after their repenting to John. Instead, John put them into the water to bury them, indicating that they were good for nothing.

The first thought of the New Testament gospel is that every fallen man of the flesh is good for nothing except death and burial, and the second thought is that if you recognize this, Jesus Christ will come to baptize you into the living God, joining you to God in resurrection. This saves you by justifying you according to His righteousness. The Baptizer, Christ, joins you to God to make you one with God, who is righteousness. God would justify you only by His righteousness. (*The God-man Living*, pp. 46-47)

Today's Reading

The base for Jesus to be baptized is that He considered Himself, according to His humanity, a man, especially an Israelite, who is a man "in the flesh" (John 1:14). Even though He was only "in the likeness of the flesh of sin" (Rom. 8:3), "without sin" (Heb. 4:15), yet He was "in the flesh," which has nothing good but is worthy only of death and burial. Christ as the Word of God became flesh....This was His standing in His humanity. John the Baptist came out to preach repentance to people in the flesh. Jesus admitted He was in the flesh. Whatever He had according to the flesh was only good for death and burial....That ground became His base for Him to be baptized.

At the beginning of His ministry for God, Jesus was willing to be baptized by John the Baptist, recognizing that, according to His humanity, He was one who did not have any qualification to be a servant of God....As a man in the flesh, He needed to be a dead man buried in the death water to fulfill...God's righteousness. (*The God-man Living,* p. 50)

You are a God-man. You have God living in you, making His home in you. You and He, He and you, are mingled together as one. You should not live a life by your natural life, your natural man. You and I, the old man, the natural man, have been terminated on the cross, crucified by the Lord in His death (Gal. 2:20a). We must leave our natural man on the cross....[Then we] will be conformed to the death of Christ (Phil. 3:10).

The death of Christ means that when Christ lived on this earth, He was always rejecting Himself. He told us that He never did anything by Himself, but He did everything by the Father (John 6:57; 5:19; 4:34; 17:4; 14:10, 24; 5:30; 7:18). He had a very holy, pure human life, but He did not live that life. He put that life aside, put that life to death, and lived by the Father's life. That was a model to us. We should be the mass production of that model, the God-men who have both the human life uplifted in Christ's resurrection and the divine life. Even our human life has been uplifted in Christ's resurrection, but we should not live by that, by ourselves.

Paul said, "I am crucified with Christ; and it is no longer I who live, but it is Christ who lives in me...and the life which I now live in the flesh I live in faith, the faith of the Son of God" (Gal. 2:20). Paul was a person living not by himself but by the pneumatic Christ, ...the all-inclusive Spirit, who is the consummation of the processed and consummated Triune God. All of this is in resurrection. When you do not live by your natural life, but live by the divine life within you, you are in resurrection. The issue of this is the Body of Christ. (*The Practical Points concerning Blending,* pp. 26-27)

Further Reading: The God-man Living, msgs. 4-6; *The Practical Points concerning Blending,* chs. 2-4

Enlightenment and inspiration: _____

WEEK 10 — DAY 6

Morning Nourishment

1 Cor. 15:10 But by the grace of God I am what I am; and His grace unto me did not turn out to be in vain, but, on the contrary, I labored more abundantly than all of them, yet not I but the grace of God which is with me.

58 Therefore, my beloved brothers, be steadfast, immovable, always abounding in the work of the Lord, knowing that your labor is not in vain in the Lord.

The believers serve and worship God, and they work and labor for the Lord. In 1 Corinthians 16:10 Paul says of Timothy, "He is working the work of the Lord, even as I am."...[Read 15:58 above.] The context of this verse is Paul's dealing with the matter of resurrection (15:1-58). Disbelief in the truth of resurrection disappoints us concerning our future, thus discouraging us in the work for the Lord. Faith gives us a strong aspiration that we may abound in the work of the Lord with the expectation of pleasing the Lord in resurrection at His coming back. (*The Conclusion of the New Testament*, p. 1839)

Today's Reading

The believers work and labor for the Lord by the Lord's resurrection life and power. Because 1 Corinthians 15 deals thoroughly and absolutely with the matter of resurrection, Paul's word in verse 58 implies resurrection life and resurrection power. Our work and labor for the Lord is not by our natural life and natural ability but by the Lord's resurrection life and power.

First Corinthians 15:10 indicates how Paul worked and labored for the Lord by His resurrection life and power....Grace, mentioned three times in this verse, is actually the resurrected Christ becoming the life-giving Spirit (v. 45) to bring the processed God in resurrection into us to be our life and life supply that we may live in resurrection. Thus, grace is the Triune God becoming life and everything to us. It was by this grace that Saul of Tarsus, the foremost of sinners (1 Tim. 1:15-16), became the foremost apostle laboring more abundantly than all the other apostles. His ministry and living by this grace are an undeniable testimony to Christ's resurrection.

"Not I, but the grace of God" equals "not I, but Christ" in Galatians 2:20. The grace that motivates the apostle and operates in him is not some matter or thing but a living person, the resurrected Christ, the embodiment of the Triune God becoming the all-inclusive life-giving Spirit, who dwells in him as his everything. By this grace Paul could be what he was and labor more abundantly than all the other apostles....We can testify that He lives in us, enabling us to do what we could never do in ourselves.

In 1 Corinthians 15:58 Paul encourages us by saying that our "labor is not in vain in the Lord." Our labor for the Lord in His resurrection life with His resurrection power will never be in vain, but will result in fulfilling God's eternal purpose through preaching Christ to sinners, ministering life to the saints, and building up the church with the experiences of the processed Triune God as gold, silver, and precious stones (1 Cor. 3:12), and will be rewarded by the returning Lord in the day of the resurrection of the righteous (1 Cor. 3:14; Matt. 25:21, 23; Luke 14:14).

We need to realize that 1 Corinthians 15:58 speaks of something in resurrection and is closely related to resurrection. If we are in resurrection, this verse applies to us. But if we are not in resurrection, we may have the mistaken idea that this verse encourages us to strive and to be energetic. The fact that this verse is related to resurrection is indicated by the word "therefore" at the beginning of the verse....Based upon what he has written in 15:1-57, Paul encourages the believers...[v. 58]. According to the natural life, we can be shaken even by a small thing.... Resurrection makes us steadfast, immovable, and always abounding in the work of the Lord. Furthermore, it causes us to know that our labor in the Lord is not in vain....In resurrection our labor in the Lord is not vain. Therefore, resurrection is not only an encouragement; it also motivates us to the work of the Lord. (*The Conclusion of the New Testament*, pp. 1839-1841)

Further Reading: The Conclusion of the New Testament, msg. 169; *Authority and Submission*, ch. 15

Enlightenment and inspiration: _____
_____
_____

Hymns, #908

1. Not of letters, but of spirit,
    The New Testamental way;
  For 'tis life the spirit giveth,
    But the letters always slay.
  Outward work God never reckons,
    But what's from the inmost part;
  It is not to serve in letter,
    But life's newness to impart.

2. Not just by the outward teachings,
    But by His anointing moved;
  Not just by the outward pattern,
    But by inward vision proved.
  Not by human rules or rituals,
    But by heaven's rule within;
  Not by human-made decisions,
    But by guidance giv'n of Him.

3. Not a dead religion serving,
    But in Christ as life to live;
  Not theology dispensing,
    But a living Christ to give.
  Not the knowledge of mere doctrine,
    But the message Christ should be;
  Not the gifts, the forms, the teachings,
    But God's Christ—reality.

4. Not objectively to worship,
    But to serve Him inwardly;
  Not to preach a Christ objective,
    But Himself subjectively.
  Not just by the Scripture serving,
    But in spirit and in life;
  Not by flesh, but by the Spirit
    Filling, freeing from all strife.

WEEK 10 — PROPHECY

Composition for prophecy with main point and sub-points:

WEEK 11 — OUTLINE

The Faith as the Gospel and the Goal of the Gospel

Scripture Reading: Gal. 1:23; 6:10; 1 Tim. 1:4; Jude 3; Matt. 26:6-13

Day 1

I. Like Paul, we should announce the faith as the gospel (Gal. 1:23):
  A. The faith is the contents of the complete gospel according to God's New Testament economy; hence, it is objective (1 Tim. 1:19; 2:7; 3:9; 4:1, 6; 5:8; 6:10, 12, 21; 2 Tim. 3:8; 4:7; Titus 1:13):
    1. The faith denotes the contents of the New Testament as our faith, in which we believe for our salvation (Acts 6:7; 1 Tim. 6:21; 2 Tim. 2:18).
    2. In Galatians 1:23 *the faith* implies our believing in Christ, taking His person and His redemptive work as the object of our faith.
  B. Faith refers to the act of believing in the gospel, in God, and in His word and deeds; hence, it is subjective (1 Tim. 1:2, 4-5, 14, 19; 2:15; 2 Tim. 1:5; 2:22).

Day 2

  C. Galatians gives us a revelation of the faith as the gospel in certain basic principles (1:11-12, 23; 2:5, 14):
    1. Fallen man cannot be justified out of works of law (v. 16a).
    2. Under God's New Testament economy we are not to keep the law; rather, we are justified out of faith in Christ (v. 16b).
    3. We are dead to the law, we are alive to God, and we have Christ living in us (vv. 19-20).
    4. In God's New Testament economy we have life and live by faith (3:11).
    5. The gospel was preached to Abraham; the New Testament economy is a continuation of God's dealing with Abraham (vv. 8-14).
    6. We receive the promise of the Spirit through faith (v. 14).
    7. In Christ we are a new creation (6:15).

D. God's economy is initiated and developed in the sphere of faith; faith is the unique way for God to carry out His New Testament economy with His chosen and redeemed people (1 Tim. 1:4; Heb. 11:6).

Day 3

E. The objective faith produces subjective faith (Gal. 1:23; 2:20; 3:1-2, 5):
  1. Faith is a matter of seeing a view of the contents of God's New Testament economy (Heb. 12:2).
  2. Because we have seen a revelation regarding the contents of God's economy, we spontaneously believe in what we see (Eph. 3:9).

F. Through the faith as the gospel, we are members of the household of the faith; this household is composed of all who are sons of God through faith in Christ Jesus (Gal. 6:10; 3:26).

G. We should hold the mystery of the faith—the things which constitute the gospel—in a pure conscience (1 Tim. 3:9):
  1. The mystery of the faith is mainly Christ as the mystery of God and the church as the mystery of Christ (Col. 2:2; Eph. 3:4).
  2. A serving one should hold the mystery of the faith with full understanding in a pure conscience for the Lord's testimony (1 Tim. 3:9).

H. To keep the faith is to keep the entire New Testament economy of God—the faith concerning Christ as the embodiment of God and the mystery of God and the church as the Body of Christ and the mystery of Christ (2 Tim. 4:7c).

I. The faith has been delivered once for all to the saints, and for this faith we should contend (Jude 3).

J. We need to arrive at the oneness of the faith; the speciality of the church is the faith, which is composed of our beliefs concerning the Bible, God, Christ, the work of Christ, salvation, and the church (Eph. 4:13).

K. On the foundation of our most holy faith and in the sphere of it, we need to build up ourselves; as we build ourselves up in our most holy faith, we

WEEK 11 — OUTLINE

build ourselves up in a faith that is both objective and subjective (Jude 20).

Day 4

II. **The goal of the gospel is that, like Mary, who did "what she could," we would pour out upon the Lord Jesus what is most precious to us, even our most costly and valuable spiritual treasure, "wasting" ourselves upon Him (Matt. 26:6-13; Mark 14:3-9):**

A. Being grateful to the Lord and loving Him, Simon the leper spread a feast in his house for the Lord and His disciples in order to enjoy His presence; a saved sinner would always do this (Matt. 26:6-7).

B. The gospel of God causes genuine believers to have a great change in their concept of value; whereas others reject the Lord, we treasure Him and value His surpassing worth and supreme preciousness (Mark 14:3; Matt. 26:7; 1 Pet. 2:4, 6-7).

C. Mary received the revelation of the Lord's death through His words, and thus she grasped the opportunity to pour out upon the Lord the best that she had; to love the Lord with our best requires a revelation concerning Him (Matt. 26:2, 12; 16:21; 17:22-23; 20:18-19).

Day 5

D. The Lord desires that we allow Him to have the first place in all things (Mark 14:7):

1. The Lord Jesus should have the first place, the preeminence, in our love, in our tripartite being, in our Christian life and church life, and in everything in our personal universe (12:30; 14:7; Col. 1:18; 3:4, 11, 17).

2. To give the Lord the first place in all things is to love Him with the first love, the best love; in order to give Him the preeminence, we must be willing to be adjusted, to be broken, and to be made nothing so that the Lord can have a way in us, through us, and among us for the building up of His Body (Rev. 2:4; Gal. 6:3; Eph. 4:16).

E. We must love the Lord Jesus and grasp the opportunity to love Him; to love the Lord is to

appreciate Him, to direct our being toward Him, to open to Him, to enjoy Him, to give Him the first place, to be one with Him, to live Him, and to become Him (Matt. 26:11; 2 Cor. 3:16; Mark 12:30; Col. 1:18; 1 Cor. 6:17; Phil. 1:20-21a; S. S. 6:13).
F. Mary did "what she could"; this means that she gave up her all, lavished all on the Lord, and kept nothing in reserve (Mark 14:8a).

Day 6

G. Mary anointed the Lord's body "beforehand for the burial" (v. 8b):
  1. The word *beforehand* introduces the factor of time that should cause us to consider if, in our love for the Lord, we are pouring out our best upon Him today.
  2. When we see the Lord face to face, we will love Him as never before, and we will pour out everything for Him, but it will be the most blessed for those who have poured out their all upon the Lord today (Matt. 26:7; Mark 14:3; John 12:3).
H. The disciples considered Mary's love offering to the Lord a "waste," but the Lord intends that the gospel should cause believers to come to Him and "waste" themselves on Him (Mark 14:4; Matt. 26:8 and footnote 1).
I. "Wherever this gospel is proclaimed in the whole world, what this woman has done shall also be told as a memorial of her" (v. 13):
  1. "This gospel" refers to the gospel of the Lord's death, burial, and resurrection (Mark 14:9; 1 Cor. 15:1-4).
  2. The story of the gospel is that the Lord loved us, and the story of Mary is that she loved the Lord (Matt. 26:13; Gal. 2:20; Mark 12:30):
    a. We must preach both the Lord loving us and us loving the Lord; one is for our salvation, and the other is for our consecration (John 3:16; 2 Cor. 5:14-15).
    b. The gospel tells us how the Lord loved us,

but the loving story of Mary stirs up our love for the Lord; thus, there needs to be a mutual love, and this must accompany the preaching of the gospel (Matt. 26:13).

Morning Nourishment

Gal. But they only heard *this:* He who was formerly perse-
1:23 cuting us is now announcing as the gospel the faith which formerly he ravaged.

2 Tim. I have fought the good fight; I have finished the course;
4:7 I have kept the faith.

1 Tim. Holding faith and a good conscience, *concerning*
1:19 which some, thrusting *these* away, have become shipwrecked regarding the faith.

In Ephesians 4:13-14 the "wind of teaching" and "the oneness of the faith" are mentioned. The faith is the contents of the complete gospel according to God's New Testament economy. Whatever the Lord spoke in the four Gospels and whatever He continued to speak in the Acts and in the Epistles through the apostles is the faith. The very contents of the New Testament Bible are the very contents of God's New Testament economy as the faith in which we have our belief. We all need to arrive at this faith, so we should not stress the different winds of different teachings. If you would be carried about by the winds of teaching, this indicates that you are still a little child according to Ephesians 4:14.

We are not for the teachings which can be considered as winds, but we are for the oneness of the unique faith which is the very contents of God's New Testament economy. (*Elders' Training, Book 7: One Accord for the Lord's Move,* pp. 42-43)

Today's Reading

The speciality of the church life is *the faith.* In the New Testament the word *faith* is used with two different meanings. First, it means the action of believing (Rom. 5:1; Eph. 2:8; Heb. 11:1). We have faith in the Lord Jesus, and this is the action of believing. This is the subjective meaning of the word faith. There is also the second meaning, that is, the objective meaning of the word faith. Faith used in this way refers to the things in which we believe, the object of our faith, our belief (Titus 1:4; Rev. 14:12; 2 Tim. 4:7). So when we say the speciality of the church life is the faith, we mean the faith which is the object of our believing. This is what we call our Christian faith. As Christians we have a unique faith. Paul said he fought the good fight and kept the faith (2 Tim. 4:7), and he also charged Timothy to fight the good fight of the faith (1 Tim. 6:12). Jude told us to contend for the faith which was once delivered to the saints (Jude 3). The faith mentioned in these verses...refers to the things in which we believe for our salvation and for the church life....Thus, the faith is something unique, something specific, something special. Therefore, in the church life we have only one thing that is specific or special. That is *the faith,* our Christian faith, which is composed of the beliefs concerning the Bible, God, Christ, the work of Christ, salvation, and the church. (*The Speciality, Generality, and Practicality of the Church,* pp. 7-8)

Faith in Galatians 1:23 and in 3:2, 5, 7, 9, 23, 25, and 6:10 implies our believing in Christ, taking His person and His redemptive work as the object of our faith. This...[is] the principle of God's dealing with people in the New Testament. This faith characterizes the believers in Christ and distinguishes them from the keepers of law. (*Life-study of Galatians,* p. 122)

[First Timothy 1:19 says, "Holding faith and a good conscience, concerning which some, thrusting these away, have become shipwrecked regarding the faith."] To keep faith and a good conscience is a safeguard for our Christian faith and life. The word *shipwrecked* implies that the Christian life and the church life are like a ship sailing on a stormy sea, needing to be safeguarded by faith and a good conscience.

Those who thrust away faith and a good conscience become shipwrecked regarding *the* faith. In this verse Paul speaks both of subjective faith, our act of believing, and of objective faith, those things in which we believe. In speaking of those who are shipwrecked regarding the faith, Paul has in mind the objective faith, the contents of the complete gospel according to God's New Testament economy. (*Life-study of 1 Timothy,* p. 22)

Further Reading: *Life-study of Galatians,* msgs. 2, 6, 14; *The Speciality, Generality, and Practicality of the Church,* ch. 1

Enlightenment and inspiration: _____

WEEK 11 — DAY 2

Morning Nourishment

Gal. ...I make known to you, brothers, *concerning* the gos-
1:11-12 pel announced by me, that it is not according to man. For neither did I receive it from man, nor was I taught it, but *I received it* through a revelation by Jesus Christ.

Heb. ...Without faith it is impossible to be well pleasing *to*
11:6 *Him,* for he who comes forward to God must believe that He is and that He is a rewarder of those who diligently seek Him.

Faith is the unique requirement for man to contact God in His New Testament economy (Heb. 11:6). Law is related to the flesh (Rom. 7:5) and depends on the effort of the flesh, the very flesh that is the expression of "I." Faith is related to the Spirit, and trusts in the operation of the Spirit, the very Spirit who is the realization of Christ....To receive the Spirit by faith is God's revealed way; it is in the light of God's revelation and issues in life and glory (Rom. 8:2, 6, 10-11, 30). Hence, we must treasure faith, not the works of law. It is by the hearing of faith that we have received the Spirit that we may participate in God's promised blessing and live Christ. (*Life-study of Galatians,* p. 120)

Today's Reading

Although Galatians is a short book, it affords us a complete revelation of the reality of the gospel. This revelation, however, is given not in detail, but in certain basic principles.

The first aspect of the truth of the gospel is that fallen man cannot be justified by works of law....Paul declares, "Out of the works of law no flesh will be justified" [2:16]. The word flesh here means fallen man who has become flesh (Gen. 6:3). No such man will be justified by works of law.

Under God's New Testament economy, we are not to keep the law. On the contrary, we are justified by faith in Christ (Gal. 2:16). We may be so familiar with the expression "justified out of faith in Christ" that we take it for granted....Faith in Christ denotes an organic union through believing. The proper preaching of the gospel is not the preaching of a doctrine; it is the preaching of the person of the Son of God.

In God's New Testament economy, man also has life by faith and lives by faith. In 3:11 Paul says, "The righteous one shall have life and live by faith."...As a result of the organic union, we have life in us. Furthermore, we live by the faith which is our appreciation of the precious Lord Jesus. We not only have life, but we also live by this life.

In 2:19 Paul says, "For I through law have died to law that I might live to God." It is very difficult to explain in doctrine what it means to die to the law so that we might live to God. It is most helpful to consider this matter in the light of our experience. Our Christian experience proves that as soon as our organic union with Christ took place, we had the sense that we were dead to the world, to sin, to the self, and to all the obligations of the law. At the same time, we were conscious of the fact that we were alive to God.

Another aspect of the truth of the gospel is that in Christ man is to be a new creation. Galatians 6:15 says, "For neither is circumcision anything nor uncircumcision, but a new creation is what matters." The new creation is the mingling of God with man.

In Galatians 3 Paul says that the word spoken to Abraham... was the gospel preached to Abraham....Paul came to see that what God had spoken to Abraham was not just a promise or merely a covenant ratified and confirmed, but that it was the very gospel. In this covenant, Paul learned, the main items of the new testament gospel were included. Thus, the covenant ratified with Abraham was a forerunner of the new covenant, of the new testament.

Faith in Christ brings us into the blessing God promised to Abraham, which is the promise of the Spirit. The believing ones are justified by faith, and they have life and live by faith. As justified ones, we live by the organic union and participate in the all-inclusive life-giving Spirit. This Spirit is the blessing of the gospel. (*Life-study of Galatians,* pp. 69, 72, 75-76, 146, 151)

Further Reading: Life-study of Galatians, msgs. 8, 15-17, 19

Enlightenment and inspiration: _____

WEEK 11 — DAY 3

Morning Nourishment

Jude 3 Beloved, while using all diligence to write to you concerning our common salvation, I found it necessary to write to you *and* exhort *you* to earnestly contend for the faith once for all delivered to the saints.

20 But you, beloved, building up yourselves upon your most holy faith, praying in the Holy Spirit.

1 Tim. 3:9 Holding the mystery of the faith in a pure conscience.

The faith [in Jude 20] is objective faith and refers to the precious things of the New Testament in which we believe for our salvation in Christ.

It is correct to say that faith in verse 20 is objective faith. However, we need to realize that this objective faith produces subjective faith. Faith first refers to the truth contained in the Word of God and conveyed by the Word. The written word of God in the Bible and the spoken word in the genuine and proper preaching and teaching contain the truth and convey the truth to us. By truth we mean the reality of what God is, the reality of the process through which God has passed, and the reality of what He has accomplished, attained, and obtained. (*Life-study of Jude*, p. 17)

Today's Reading

As we listen to the word that contains the truth, the Spirit of Christ works within us. The Spirit of Christ always works according to the Word and with the Word. This means that the Spirit of Christ cooperates with the Word. As a result of this cooperation, eventually in our experience there is a "click," like that made by the shutter of a camera, and the "scene" of what is contained in the Word is impressed on our spirit and becomes our faith....This is the faith allotted to us as our portion from God (2 Pet. 1:1), and this portion is nothing less than the New Testament inheritance.

This faith is both objective and subjective. As we build ourselves up upon our most holy faith, we build ourselves up in a faith that is not only objective but especially subjective. The subjective faith comes out of the objective faith....This is the most holy faith. (*Life-study of Jude*, p. 18)

Faith is a matter of seeing a view of the contents of God's New Testament economy. Once we have the view, we shall believe in what we see. This faith is the foundation of our Christian life. Out of our faith love will flow forth. In the church life we are living a life of love. We should love everyone: those believers who meet with us and those who do not and also the unbelievers. This love is the issue of our faith. Furthermore, we shall then have a life that is full of hope. We are living for Christ, we are expressing Him, and we are even His Body. As we wait for His coming back, we are filled with hope. Our hope, destiny, and destination are not on this earth. They are altogether focused on the coming back of the Lord Jesus.

In the meetings of the church and of the ministry, it is as if we are all watching a heavenly television to see more of God's economy. The more we see this heavenly television, the more we believe. We spontaneously believe in what we see. Therefore, we come away from meetings full of the ability to believe. The meetings of the church and the ministry enlarge our capacity to believe. (*Life-study of 1 Thessalonians*, pp. 127, 122-123)

The faith [in 1 Timothy 3:9], as in 1:19 and 2 Timothy 4:7, is objective. It refers to the things we believe in, the things which constitute the gospel. The mystery of the faith is mainly Christ as the mystery of God (Col. 2:2) and the church as the mystery of Christ (Eph. 3:4). A deacon in a local church should hold this mystery with full understanding in a pure conscience for the Lord's testimony. (*Life-study of 1 Timothy*, p. 49)

Paul could testify that he had kept the faith. This means that he kept God's New Testament economy. To keep the faith is to keep the entire New Testament economy of God—the faith concerning Christ as the embodiment of God and the mystery of God and the church as the Body of Christ and the mystery of Christ. (*Life-study of 2 Timothy*, p. 62)

Further Reading: Life-study of Jude, msgs. 1, 3; Life-study of 1 Thessalonians, msg. 14; The Conclusion of the New Testament, msg. 171

Enlightenment and inspiration: _____

Morning Nourishment

Matt. 26:6-8 ...When Jesus was in Bethany, in the house of Simon the leper, a woman came to Him, having an alabaster flask of ointment of great value, and she poured *it* on His head as He reclined *at table*. But when the disciples saw *it*, they were indignant, saying, Why this waste?

12 For in pouring out this ointment on My body, she has done *it* for My burial.

Although the religionists hated the Lord Jesus [Matt. 26:3-5], His disciples loved Him (vv. 6-13). Two of those who loved Him were Simon the leper and Mary, the woman who poured the oil upon His head. A leper signifies a sinner (8:2). Simon, as a leper, must have been healed by the Lord. Being grateful to the Lord and loving Him, he spread a feast (26:7) in his house for the Lord and His disciples in order to enjoy His presence. A saved sinner would always do this. Simon must have known that the Lord was about to be killed. He probably realized that this was the last opportunity for him to express his love to the Lord. Therefore, he grasped the opportunity for a further intimate, loving contact with the Lord. He opened his home, spread a feast, and invited the Lord and all those who loved Him. (*Life-study of Matthew*, p. 785)

Today's Reading

[In Matthew 26:6-8] the disciples considered Mary's love offering to the Lord a waste. Throughout the past twenty centuries, thousands of precious lives, heart treasures, high positions, and golden futures have been wasted upon the Lord Jesus. To such lovers He is altogether lovely and worthy of their offering. What they have poured upon Him is not a waste, but a fragrant testimony of His sweetness.

In verse 11 the Lord said to the indignant disciples, "For the poor you have with you always, but you do not always have Me." This indicates that we must love the Lord and grasp the opportunity to express our love to Him. Verse 12 says, "For in pouring out this ointment on My body, she has done it for My burial." Mary received the revelation of the Lord's death by the Lord's words in

16:21; 17:22-23; 20:18-19; and 26:2. Hence, she grasped the opportunity to pour the best she had upon the Lord. To love the Lord with our best requires a revelation concerning Him.

Along with Simon, Mary also probably thought that this was her last chance to do something over the Lord's body to anoint Him for burial. In a very real sense, Mary buried the Lord Jesus before He was crucified. What a contrast there is between the religionists who hated the Lord and wanted to kill Him and His lovers who took the opportunity to express their love for Him! I believe that the others like Peter, James, and John did not receive the Lord's prophecy concerning His crucifixion properly. According to the Lord's testimony, Mary certainly received His word regarding this, for the Lord testified that in pouring out the ointment, she had done it for His burial. This was a sign that Mary understood what the Lord had prophesied concerning His crucifixion. (*Life-study of Matthew*, pp. 785-786)

Have our eyes been opened to see the preciousness of the One whom we are serving? Have we come to see that nothing less than the dearest, the costliest, the most precious, is fit for Him?

The Lord has to open our eyes to His worth. If there is in the world some precious art treasure, and I pay the high price asked for it, be it one thousand, ten thousand, or even fifty thousand pounds, dare anyone say it is a waste? The idea of waste only comes into our Christianity when we underestimate the worth of our Lord. The whole question is: How precious is He to us now? If we do not think much of Him, then of course to give Him anything at all, however small, will seem to us a wicked waste. But when He is really precious to our souls, nothing will be too good, nothing too costly for Him; everything we have, our dearest, our most priceless treasure, we shall pour out upon Him, and we shall not count it a shame to have done so. ("The Normal Christian Life," *The Collected Works of Watchman Nee*, vol. 33, p. 193)

Further Reading: Life-study of Matthew, msg. 68; *The Collected Works of Watchman Nee*, vol. 60, ch. 45

Enlightenment and inspiration: _____

WEEK 11 — DAY 5

Morning Nourishment

Mark 12:30 "...You shall love the Lord your God from your whole heart and from your whole soul and from your whole mind and from your whole strength."

Col. 1:18 And He is the Head of the Body, the church; He is the beginning, the Firstborn from the dead, that He Himself might have the first place in all things.

Eph. 6:24 Grace be with all those who love our Lord Jesus Christ in incorruptibility.

Christ has the preeminence in all things [Col. 1:18]....If we would allow Him to have the preeminence in all things and in everything, then we will be blessed. We should let Him have the preeminence in everything: in our married life, in our family life, in our parent-child relationships, in our buying and selling of property, in our bank accounts, in our education, and in all our business affairs. Christ should have the first place in all things. (*Christ in His Excellency*, p. 14)

Today's Reading

Philippians is a book on the experience of Christ. Hence, even the exaltation of Christ in this book is related to our experience. When I was young, I was taught about Christ's exaltation. However, I did not see much of Christ's exaltation in the lives of believers. This was primarily just a teaching from the Bible. We need to experience Christ to such a high degree that in our life He is exalted. ...God has already exalted Christ in the universe, but now it remains for us to exalt Him in our personal universe—in our daily life, in our family life, and in our church life. (*Life-study of Philippians*, p. 95)

We need to see that in the seven epistles to the churches in Revelation 2 and 3, the first dealing of the Lord is concerning the recovery of the first love (2:4). ...Surely we [love Him]. But do we give Him the preeminence, the first place, in all things? To give the Lord the first place in all things is to love Him with the first love, the best love. In order to give Him the preeminence, we must be willing to be adjusted, to be broken, to be made nothing, so that the Lord can have a way in us, through us, and among us for the building up of His organic Body. (*Fellowship concerning the Urgent Need of the Vital Groups,* p. 111)

Of Mary the Lord said: "She has done what she could" [Mark 14:8]. What does that mean? It means that she had given up her all. She had kept nothing in reserve for a future day. She had lavished on Him all she had; and yet on the resurrection morning she had no reason to regret her extravagance. And the Lord will not be satisfied with anything less from us than that we too should have done "what we could." By this, remember, I do not mean the expenditure of our effort and energy in trying to do something for Him, for that is not the point here. What the Lord Jesus looks for in us is a life laid at His feet, and that in view of His death and burial and of a future day. His burial was already in view that day in the home in Bethany. Today it is His crowning that is in view, when He shall be acclaimed in glory as the Anointed One, the Christ of God. Yes, then we shall pour out our all upon Him! But it is a precious thing—indeed it is a far more precious thing to Him—that we should anoint Him now, not with any material oil but with something costly, something from our hearts. ("The Normal Christian Life," *The Collected Works of Watchman Nee,* vol. 33, pp. 193-194)

We must love the Lord and seize the opportunity to love Him. Today many Christians care more for works of charity than for Christ. A charitable concern for the poor often replaces Christ. But in Mark 14 the Lord Jesus would not allow the concern for the poor to be a replacement of Himself. Here it seems that He does not care for the poor, but cares only for Himself. He seems to be saying, "Do not trouble this one who loves Me. She has done a good work on Me. If you want to take care of the poor, wait for another time and go to another place. The poor are always with you. But this is the unique time for you to take Me as your replacement and to pour out everything upon Me." (*Life-study of Mark,* pp. 367-368)

Further Reading: Life-study of Mark, msg. 42; The Conclusion of the New Testament, msg. 235

Enlightenment and inspiration: _____
_____
_____

WEEK 11 — DAY 6

Morning Nourishment

Mark 14:8 She has done what she could; she has anointed My body beforehand for the burial.

Matt. 26:13 Truly I say to you, Wherever this gospel is proclaimed in the whole world, what this woman has done shall also be told as a memorial of her.

2 Cor. 5:14 For the love of Christ constrains us...

[Mark 14:4-5 says], "But there were some who were indignantly commenting among themselves: Why has this waste of the ointment been made? For this ointment could have been sold for over three hundred denarii and given to the poor."

What is waste? Waste means, among other things, giving more than is necessary....If two grams will do and you give a kilogram, it is a waste. If three days will suffice to finish a task well enough and you lavish five days or a week on it, it is a waste. Waste means that you give something too much for something too little. If someone is receiving more than he is considered to be worth, then that is waste.

But remember, [in verses 4-9] we are dealing...with something which the Lord said was to go out with the Gospel, wherever that Gospel should be carried. Why? Because He intends that the preaching of the Gospel should issue in something along the very lines of the action of Mary here, namely, that people should come to Him and waste themselves on Him. This is the result that He is seeking.

When once our eyes have been opened to the real worth of our Lord Jesus, *nothing* is too good for Him. ("The Normal Christian Life," *The Collected Works of Watchman Nee*, vol. 33, pp. 186, 188)

Today's Reading

In Mark 14:6-8 the Lord Jesus introduces a time-factor with the word *beforehand,* and this is something of which we can have a new application today, for it is as important to us now as it was to her then. We all know that in the age to come we shall be called to a greater work—not to inactivity. "Well done, good and faithful slave. You were faithful over a few things; I will set you over many things. Enter into the joy of your master" (Matt. 25:21; and compare Matt.

24:47 and Luke 19:17). Yes, there will be a greater work; for the work of God's house will go on, just as in the story the care of the poor went on. The poor would always be with them, but they could not always have Him. There was something, represented by this pouring out of the ointment, which Mary had to do *beforehand* or she would have no later opportunity. I believe that in that day we shall all love Him as we have never done now, but yet that it will be most blessed for those who have poured out their all upon the Lord today. When we see Him face to face, I trust that we shall all break and pour out everything for Him. But *today*—what are we doing *today*?

There cannot be a limit to our loving the Lord, our serving Him, obeying Him, and our allegiance to Him; we can never overdo these things. The Lord loves to see us loving Him in a reckless way. He loves to see us loving Him beyond reason and against human affection. To Him, the gospel should result in men's being constrained by His death to love Him, consecrate to Him, and fully obey Him to the point that others would consider them *extreme*. (*The Collected Works of Watchman Nee*, vol. 33, pp. 192-193; vol. 19, p. 603)

Matthew 26:13 says, "Truly I say to you, Wherever this gospel is proclaimed in the whole world, what this woman has done shall also be told as a memorial of her." In the foregoing verse, the Lord spoke of His burial, implying His death and resurrection for our redemption. Hence, in this verse He called the gospel "this gospel," referring to the gospel of His death, burial, and resurrection (1 Cor. 15:1-4). The story of the gospel is that the Lord loved us, and the story of Mary is that she loved the Lord. We must preach both, the Lord loving us and us loving the Lord. One is for our salvation, and the other is for our consecration. The gospel tells us how the Lord loved us, but the loving story of Mary stirs us up to love the Lord. Thus, there needs to be a mutual love. This must accompany the preaching of the gospel. (*Life-study of Matthew*, p. 786)

Further Reading: The Collected Works of Watchman Nee, vol. 33, ch. 14; *Life-study of Song of Songs,* msg. 8

Enlightenment and inspiration: ___

WEEK 11 — HYMN

Hymns, #431

1 Thy mighty love, O God, constraineth me,
  As some strong tide it presseth on its way,
  Seeking a channel in my self-bound soul,
  Yearning to sweep all barriers away.

2 Shall I not yield to that constraining power?
  Shall I not say, O tide of love, flow in?
  My God, Thy gentleness hath conquered me,
  Life cannot be as it hath hither been.

3 Break through my nature, mighty, heavenly love,
  Clear every avenue of thought and brain,
  Flood my affections, purify my will,
  Let nothing but Thine own pure life remain.

4 Thus wholly mastered and possessed by God,
  Forth from my life, spontaneous and free,
  Shall flow a stream of tenderness and grace,
  Loving, because God loved, eternally.

WEEK 11 — PROPHECY

Composition for prophecy with main point and sub-points:

WEEK 12 — OUTLINE

The Genuine, Intrinsic, Highest, and Fullest Gospel of God's Economy

Scripture Reading: 2 Sam. 7:12-14a; Eph. 3:16-19; Rom. 1:1-4; 8:6, 10-11, 28-29; 12:5; 16:20

Day 1

I. **The genuine, intrinsic, highest, and fullest gospel is the gospel of God's economy—the gospel of sonship for the building up of the church as the Body of Christ by the building of God into man and man into God (1 Tim. 1:3-4; Eph. 3:8-11, 16-19; Rom. 1:3-4; 8:29; 12:5; 2 Sam. 7:12-14a):**
   A. We must believe that there is a God-created ability within man to receive and understand His gospel (Job 32:8; Zech. 12:1; Eccl. 3:11):
      1. We should not preach a gospel that has been lowered down to what we think is the level of people's understanding; we should preach an uplifted gospel and never lower the concept (1 Thes. 1:1, 3-4, 10; 5:23; 1 Cor. 2:7-13).
      2. Man was created for God, and within man there is the ability to understand the things of God, and there is a hunger for these things (Acts 17:26-31; Isa. 43:7).
   B. We must present the truth concerning the economy of God item by item according to the entire Bible; this is the Lord's special commission to us (1 Cor. 1:9; 9:16-17, 23; 1 Tim. 1:3-4; 2:7; 4:16; 2 Tim. 1:11; 2:2, 15; Col. 1:28).

Day 2

II. **The gospel of God's eternal economy is "the gospel of the promise made to the fathers" (Acts 13:32)—the promise that the seed of David would become the Son of God, that is, that a human seed would become a divine Son (vv. 22-23, 33-34; 26:6, 16-19; 2 Sam. 7:12-14a; Rom. 1:3-4; Matt. 22:41-45).**

WEEK 12 — OUTLINE

III. *The seed of David becoming the Son of God speaks of the process of Christ's being designated the firstborn Son of God by resurrection (Rom. 8:29):*
   A. Paul said that he was separated unto the gospel of God concerning God's Son, which indicates that the gospel of God is the gospel of sonship for the reality of the Body of Christ in the local churches (1:1, 3-4; 8:28-30; 12:5; 16:20).
   B. Romans 1:3-4 is the fulfillment of the prophecy in typology in 2 Samuel 7:12-14a, unveiling the mystery of God becoming man so that man may become God in life and in nature but not in the Godhead.
   C. By incarnation Christ, the only begotten Son of God in His divinity (John 1:18), put on the flesh, the human nature, which had nothing to do with divinity; in His humanity He was not the Son of God.
   D. In resurrection His humanity was deified, sonized, meaning that He was designated the Son of God, becoming the firstborn Son of God with both divinity and humanity (Rom. 8:29).
   E. Thus, in Christ God was constituted into man, man was constituted into God, and God and man were mingled together to be one entity, the God-man.
   F. God's gospel and His intention in His economy are to build God into man and man into God; this building is God becoming a man (the seed of David) that man might become God (the Son of God).
   G. This gospel was spoken by the Lord Jesus when He said, "Truly, truly, I say to you, Unless the grain of wheat falls into the ground and dies, it abides alone; but if it dies, it bears much fruit" (John 12:24):
      1. If a seed dies by being buried in the soil, it will eventually sprout, grow, and blossom in resurrection, because the operation of the

Day 3

seed's life is activated simultaneously with its death (1 Cor. 15:36; 1 Pet. 3:18).
2. The divinity, the Spirit of holiness, in Christ became operative in His death, and in resurrection He "blossomed" to be the firstborn Son of God and the life-dispensing Spirit, imparting His divine life into us to make us His many brothers (Rom. 1:4; 8:29; 1 Cor. 15:45b).
3. The prototype is the firstborn Son of God, and the reproduction is the many sons of God, the members of the prototype to be His Body, which consummates in the New Jerusalem (Col. 1:18; 1 Pet. 1:3).

Day 4
IV. **The seed of David becoming the Son of God speaks also of the process of our being designated the many sons of God by resurrection (Heb. 2:10-11):**
A. Christ has already been designated the Son of God, but we are still in the process of designation, the process of being sonized, deified (Rom. 8:28-29).
B. The life of the Son of God has been implanted into our spirit (v. 10):
1. Now we, like the seed that is sown into the earth, must pass through the process of death and resurrection (John 12:24-26).
2. This causes the outer man to be consumed, but it enables the inner life to grow, to develop, and ultimately, to blossom from within us; this is resurrection (1 Cor. 15:31, 36; 2 Cor. 4:10-12, 16-18).
C. In resurrection Christ in His humanity was designated the Son of God, and by means of such a resurrection we also are in the process of being designated sons of God (Rom. 8:11):
1. The process of our being designated, sonized, deified, is the process of resurrection with four main aspects—sanctification,

transformation, conformation, and glorification (6:22; 12:2; 8:29-30).

Day 5

2. The key to the process of designation is resurrection, which is the indwelling Christ as the rising-up Spirit, the designating Spirit, the power of life in our spirit (John 11:25; Rom. 8:10-11; Acts 2:24; 1 Cor. 15:26; 5:4):
   a. We urgently need to learn how to walk according to the spirit, to enjoy and experience the designating Spirit (Rom. 8:4, 6, 14).
   b. The more we touch the Spirit, the more we are sanctified, transformed, conformed, and glorified to become God in life and in nature but not in the Godhead for the building up of the Body of Christ to consummate the New Jerusalem (1 Cor. 12:3; Rom. 10:12-13; 8:15-16; Gal. 4:6).

D. The more we grow in life and pass through the metabolic process of transformation, the more we are designated the sons of God (2 Cor. 3:18, 6, 16; 5:4, 9, 14-15; 1:12; 12:7-9):
   1. This metabolic process is the building up of the church as the Body of Christ and the house of God by the building of God into man and man into God (Rom. 12:2; Eph. 1:22-23; 2:20-22).
   2. Humanity is designated in divinity, and divinity and humanity are blended as one; today, we, seeds of humanity, are becoming sons of God in divinity through the process of God's building.
   3. This building will consummate in the New Jerusalem as a great, corporate God-man, the aggregate, the totality, of all the sons of God (Rev. 21:7).
   4. One day this process will be completed, and for eternity we will be the same as Christ, God's firstborn Son, in our spirit, soul, and

body (1 John 3:2; Rom. 8:19, 23; *Hymns,* #948, stanza 2).

E. "On God's side, the Triune God has been incarnated to be a man; on our side, we are being deified, constituted with the processed and consummated Triune God so that we may be made God in life and in nature to be His corporate expression for eternity. This is the highest truth, and this is the highest gospel" (*Life-study of Job,* p. 122).

Day 6

V. **The genuine and intrinsic gospel is that God intends to work Himself in Christ into us (2 Sam. 7:12-14a; Rom. 1:1-4, 9):**

A. Christ builds the church by building Himself into us, making our heart, our intrinsic constitution, His home (Eph. 3:16-19).

B. If we preach this gospel, we will tell others that they need Christ, the very God Himself, to be wrought into their being (v. 17a; John 14:23).

C. "Today's world needs a crusade with the preaching of the highest and fullest gospel" (*Life-study of Hebrews,* p. 157).

WEEK 12 — DAY 1

Morning Nourishment

Rom. 1:1, 3-4 Paul, a slave of Christ Jesus, a called apostle, separated unto the gospel of God,...concerning His Son, who came out of the seed of David according to the flesh, who was designated the Son of God...

Isa. 43:6-7 ...Bring My sons from afar,...everyone who is called by My name, whom I have created, formed, and even made for My glory.

In Romans 1:1 Paul said that he was "separated unto the gospel of God," and then he goes on to say that the gospel of God concerns God's Son, Jesus Christ our Lord (1:3)....The gospel of God is a gospel of sonship. The goal of this gospel is to transform sinners into sons of God for the formation of the Body of Christ.

We are being designated sons of God through the process of resurrection. In this process a number of steps are involved. These steps include sanctification, transformation, conformation, and glorification. This glorification will also be the manifestation. Today people may not realize that we are Christians. But on the day of our glorification, no one will need to ask us whether or not we are Christians, for we shall be manifested as sons of God. That manifestation will be the consummation of the process of designation by resurrection.

We all need to serve God in the gospel of His Son. To serve God in the gospel is to serve Him not only in the matters of redemption, justification, and forgiveness, but especially in the matter of sonship. All the service in the local churches should be the service in the gospel of sonship. According to this gospel, sinners in the flesh can be transformed into sons of God in the Spirit. What glad tidings! (*Life-study of Romans*, pp. 565, 578)

Today's Reading

We must exercise our faith to preach...an uplifted gospel. We should not preach a gospel that has been lowered down to what we think is the level of people's understanding. Instead of bringing people up to the level of the gospel, many of us have lowered the thought of the gospel when presenting the truth to unbelievers....We need to realize that within man there is a God-created talent,

WEEK 12 — DAY 1

ability, to receive God and to receive and understand His gospel. Just as children are often able to understand more than their teachers realize, so unbelievers can understand more of the gospel than we realize. Whenever we preach the gospel, we must believe that those listening were created by God with a certain ability, a talent, to receive and understand the message of the gospel. We need to improve our gospel preaching. We should preach an uplifted gospel and never lower the concept.

We need to preach an uplifted gospel, a gospel that covers more than the ABC's of God's salvation. This will satisfy the hunger and thirst that is within man because of the way God created him. It will also stir up the interest of those who hear to come again to hear the preaching of the gospel. Otherwise, they may come just once.

Man was created for God, and within him there is the ability to understand the things of God, and there is a hunger for these things. Therefore, as we preach the gospel in an uplifted way, we must believe that the hearers have the ability to understand what we are saying....We need to enrich and uplift the word of our gospel preaching. (*Life-study of Exodus*, pp. 1304-1306)

The embodiment of God is Christ, the realization of Christ is the Spirit, the issue of the Spirit is the Body of Christ, and the consummation of the Body of Christ is the New Jerusalem. These five mysteries cannot be clearly explained by today's traditional theology in Christianity....The Lord's burden given to us is that we bear the testimony of His recovery, and one of the main points is to refute and correct the defects and errors of traditional Christian theology. We cannot say that traditional theology is all wrong; in fact, some of it is quite right. Nevertheless, it is incomplete.... We must present the truth concerning the economy of God item by item according to the entire Bible. This is the Lord's special commission to us. (*The Governing and Controlling Vision in the Bible*, pp. 46-47)

Further Reading: *Life-study of Romans*, msgs. 54-56; *Life-study of Exodus*, msg. 113; *The Triune God's Revelation and His Move*, msg. 12

Enlightenment and inspiration: _____

Morning Nourishment

2 Sam. 7:12-14 ...I will raise up your seed after you, which will come forth from your body, and I will establish his kingdom. It is he who will build a house for My name, and I will establish the throne of his kingdom forever. I will be his Father, and he will be My son....

Rom. 1:3-4 Concerning His Son, who came out of the seed of David according to the flesh, who was designated the Son of God in power according to the Spirit of holiness out of the resurrection of the dead, Jesus Christ our Lord.

The word [in 2 Samuel 7:12-14a] concerning "your seed" and "My son" indicates that the seed of David would become the Son of God, that the seed of a man would become God's Son.

This thought is continued very strongly in the New Testament, particularly in Romans 1:3 and 4....Here we have the same thought...—that the seed of David becomes the Son of God. These verses reveal, on the one hand, that Christ is the seed of David and, on the other hand, that He, the seed of David, has been designated the Son of God. When we compare these two portions of the Word, we see that both in the Old Testament and in the New Testament we have the matter of the seed of David becoming the Son of God. (*Life-study of 1 & 2 Samuel*, p. 165)

Today's Reading

This seed of David in His humanity was sonized, was made ("designated"—Rom. 1:4) the Son of God. Jesus in His humanity, in that part, was not the Son of God. He was of the old creation, the old man, having the flesh, which is involved with Satan, sin, and the world. So this part had to be made divine, to be sonized, designated, that it might become a part of the Son of God.

It is very hard to say what the word *designated* means in Romans 1:4. *Sonized* means to be made a son, but what is *designated*? Christ is a wonderful person. He has two parts: the man-part, the part of man, and the God-part, the part of God. The part of man is human. The part of God is divine. The human part is in the flesh, involved with the negative things, and the divine part is marvelous. How could this human part in such a flesh be made a part of the Son of God? It was in His resurrection that Christ made His humanity, divinity. His resurrection uplifted the humanity of Jesus into the level of divinity. Here is the essence of the person of Christ. This is very, very deep. Jesus' divinity is the Spirit of holiness, having the divine power and the divine element to transform Jesus' humanity, making it divine. This is what it means to designate, and this is to sonize.

This is the fulfillment of the prophecy in typology in 2 Samuel 7:12-14. In this fulfillment we have seen the essence of Christ's person as the seed of David in His humanity....The Son of God is the divine part of Christ. He was designated the Son of God in His humanity. He was the Son of Man in the flesh. How could He be the Son of God, so divine? It was by designation in resurrection.

This designation was in power according to the Spirit of holiness. The Spirit of holiness is the divinity (Rom. 9:5) in the seed of David—a man of humanity (Rom. 5:15, 17b, 19). Romans 9:5 shows us that Christ is God. As God He had divinity in Himself to be the seed of David, a man of humanity.

Jesus Christ as a man in the flesh was designated the Son of God in power according to the Spirit of holiness out of the resurrection of the dead. The resurrection is the consummation of the processed Triune God. Resurrection is a person. The Lord Jesus said, "I am the resurrection" (John 11:25a). The Triune God in eternity was just the Triune God, only divine. But He was processed through incarnation, human living, death, and resurrection. Then He was consummated to be not only divine but also human. Now He has passed through all the processes of incarnation, human living, and death. In resurrection He became the consummated Triune God, who is resurrection itself. (*Crystallization-study of the Epistle to the Romans*, pp. 9-10)

Further Reading: Life-study of 1 & 2 Samuel, msgs. 25, 27, 31; *Crystallization-study of the Epistle to the Romans*, msgs. 1-3, 18; *Life-study of 1 & 2 Chronicles*, msgs. 2, 4

Enlightenment and inspiration:

Morning Nourishment

Rom. Because those whom He foreknew, He also predesti-
8:29 nated *to be* conformed to the image of His Son, that
He might be the Firstborn among many brothers.

John ...Unless the grain of wheat falls into the ground and
12:24 dies, it abides alone; but if it dies, it bears much fruit.

Out of such a resurrection, which is the consummation of the processed Triune God, Jesus Christ as a man in the flesh was made the firstborn Son of God (Rom. 8:29). He is the Son of God, but now the Son of God is different from what the Son of God was before. When the Son of God was merely the only begotten Son of God, He had only divinity. But now He has His humanity, and His humanity has been made divine to become a part of Him as the Son of God....This Son of God is now the Firstborn of God.

An only son could never be the firstborn. Christ's being the firstborn Son indicates that many sons follow. These many sons are God's chosen people; the millions of them were all regenerated in the same resurrection (1 Pet. 1:3) in which Christ was made the Son of God in His humanity. In that big resurrection ...the human part of Christ was made divine to be sonized. At the same time, all His believers were regenerated....In His resurrection, all these human believers were made divine through the regeneration to be the many sons of God. Thus, Christ became the firstborn Son of God with many brothers.

Christ was the only begotten Son of God (John 1:18) before His incarnation, having divinity only, without humanity. Jesus Christ became the firstborn Son of God in resurrection, with His God-created humanity uplifted, having both divinity and humanity. The regenerated believers, having both humanity and divinity, are to be conformed to the image of this firstborn Son of God.

Thus, the person of Jesus Christ the God-man implies the intention of God in His gospel, that is, that He, as the unique God, wants to become a man that the fallen men redeemed by Him could become His many sons, made the same as God in His life and nature but not in His Godhead. (*Crystallization-study of the Epistle to the Romans,* pp. 10-11)

Today's Reading

In John 12:24 the Lord Jesus said that He was a grain of wheat, which unless it "falls into the ground and dies, it abides alone; but if it dies, it bears much fruit." This is to die and live, that is, to live by dying; to die is to live. Apparently a grain dies when it falls into the ground, but actually that death is for the grain to live. It is through death that the grain of wheat is activated within so that the inner life power has the opportunity to operate and bring forth new sprouts. The death of the Lord Jesus opened the shell of His flesh, and the Spirit of holiness had the great opportunity to operate for the germination of the new creation.

It is through death that life operates. The Lord Jesus was both God and man. People thought that if they killed Him, He would be finished since He was merely a man. Little did they know that His being killed afforded Him a great opportunity for the divinity in Him to become operative. It was then that He was designated in His humanity to be the Son of God by the Spirit of holiness (the divinity of Christ) in resurrection. (*The Governing and Controlling Vision in the Bible*, p. 56)

Those responsible for the crucifixion of Christ did not realize that crucifixion was the best way for Him to be designated, to be glorified. We may use a carnation seed to illustrate this point. If the seed is put to an end by being buried in the soil, it will eventually sprout, grow, and blossom. In the same principle, through death and resurrection Christ "blossomed" as the Son of God. Satan expected the crucifixion of Christ to mark His termination, but the Lord Jesus knew that this was actually the beginning, that it would lead to His designation according to the Spirit of holiness out of the resurrection from the dead. Without death, there can be no resurrection. Hallelujah, in resurrection Christ was designated the Son of God in power! (*Life-study of Romans*, p. 551)

Further Reading: The Governing and Controlling Vision in the Bible, chs. 2-4; Life-study of Romans, msg. 53; The Vital Groups, msgs. 2, 10-11

Enlightenment and inspiration: _____

Morning Nourishment

Rom. And we know that all things work together for good
8:28-29 to those who love God, to those who are called according to *His* purpose. Because those whom He foreknew, He also predestinated *to be* conformed to the image of His Son, that He might be the Firstborn among many brothers.

We have [divinity] by being regenerated in our spirit by the Spirit of Christ. Through incarnation Christ put humanity upon Himself and thereafter had two natures, the divine nature and the human nature. Through His resurrection and through coming into us as the Spirit, Christ has brought divinity into us. Therefore, we also have two natures, the human nature and the divine nature. By being born of the Spirit we have become partakers of the divine nature (2 Pet. 1:4). We can say, "Lord, just as You have two natures, so we have two natures also. You are divine and human, and we are human and divine. Hallelujah, we are the same as You! Lord, You have our nature, and we have Yours.... You are the Head of the Body, and we are the members of the Body. Lord, You are the Son of God, and we are sons of God also." The Lord...enjoys it when we declare the fact that God no longer has just one Son...but many sons, Christ as the Firstborn and us as the many sons of God. Christ has already been designated the Son of God, but we are still in the process of designation. One day this process will be completed, and for eternity we shall be the same as Christ, God's firstborn Son. Romans 1:3 and 4 contain many key words. Verse 3 has the phrase "according to the flesh," and verse 4, the phrase "according to the Spirit." In 8:4 Paul speaks about walking "according to the spirit" and not "according to the flesh." This is one example of how the key words in 1:3 and 4 are used again by Paul later in this book. (*Life-study of Romans*, pp. 551-552)

Today's Reading

In the same principle, we are designated the sons of God by a change in life through the process of resurrection. The day is coming when we shall reach the stage of "full blossom." That will be the time of the redemption, the glorification, of our body, which is the full sonship (Rom. 8:23). The life of the Son of God has been implanted into our spirit. Now we, like the carnation seed that is sown into the earth, must pass through the process of death and resurrection. This causes the outward man to be consumed, but it enables the inner life to grow, to develop, and, ultimately, to blossom. This is resurrection. Praise the Lord that we are daily being put to death so that we may share Christ's resurrection in a practical way. Hallelujah, we shall be designated sons of God by resurrection!

We are on the way of resurrection. Not only have we been grafted into Christ that we may have a vital union with Him in His death, but we also enjoy His resurrection. We all are presently in the process of being designated sons of God by means of resurrection.

In this process of resurrection there are four aspects: sanctification, transformation, conformation, and glorification. In 6:22 Paul says, "But now, having been freed from sin and enslaved to God, you have your fruit unto sanctification, and the end, eternal life." Sanctification, the process of being made holy, brings us into the enjoyment of eternal life. Thus, the end, the issue, of sanctification is eternal life.

We all have the sense within that today our sonship is not yet full. However, it will get fuller and fuller until it reaches the peak at the time of our glorification, when we shall be fully resurrected and designated the sons of God in nature and in appearance. Both in name and in reality we shall be the sons of God in spirit, in soul, and in body. Just as a carnation seed grows from a seed into a full-grown blossoming plant, so we shall be processed through resurrection until we are fully glorified and designated as the many sons of God. We are now in the process of resurrection so that we may be sanctified, transformed, conformed, and glorified. This process will go on until we are sons of God in full. This is the central aim of the gospel. (*Life-study of Romans*, pp. 553-554, 556)

Further Reading: Life-study of Romans, msg. 52; *Life-study of 1 & 2 Chronicles*, msg. 7

Enlightenment and inspiration: _____

WEEK 12 — DAY 5

Morning Nourishment

Rom. 8:10-11   But if Christ is in you, though the body is dead because of sin, the spirit is life because of righteousness. And if the Spirit of the One who raised Jesus from the dead dwells in you, He who raised Christ from the dead will also give life to your mortal bodies through His Spirit who indwells you.

When the brothers and sisters have their being according to the Spirit, they are wonderful and glorious. Whether you have your being according to the flesh or according to the Spirit depends on the choice you make....May the Lord be merciful to us so that we may choose to live according to the Spirit. We urgently need to learn how to walk according to the Spirit. If we walk according to the flesh, the church life will be most unpleasant. But if we walk according to the Spirit, the church life will be in the heavens.

The sonship is realized by resurrection and in the Spirit. The Spirit who dwells in us is the rising-up Spirit and the designating Spirit. Day by day, this Spirit is designating us the sons of God.

[Romans] reveals that we should help others not only to be saved, but also to experience the sonship. This means that we need to help them to see the matter of designation by resurrection, including sanctification, transformation, conformation, and glorification. (*Life-study of Romans*, pp. 571-572)

Today's Reading

When we enjoy...Christ by eating, drinking, and breathing Him, a metabolic process, a spiritual digestion and metabolism, takes place within us. Through this metabolic process Christ is constituted into our being. This constitution is the building. Christ, therefore, is building Himself into us as our inner constitution. The issue of such a building is that we become...the members of the Body of Christ.

In Matthew 16:18 the Lord Jesus said, "I will build My church." ...He is building His church by supplying us with spiritual drink and by feeding us with spiritual food, which are uniquely Himself as the Spirit. The more we enjoy Him by eating, drinking, and breathing Him, the more He builds His church.

WEEK 12 — DAY 5

Just as every member of our physical body is organic, so every member of the Body of Christ is organic. The church is a group of transformed people who have grown into one organism, the organic Body of Christ. The way to be built up as this organism is to grow, and the way to grow is to eat, drink, and breathe Christ. No matter what our race or nationality may be, we are all undergoing the same metabolic process that day by day produces transformation, which equals building. This is the spiritual growth and also the spiritual building. (*Life-study of 1 & 2 Samuel,* pp. 173-174)

The processed Triune God as the consummated Spirit is in our spirit. Therefore, as Christians we should remain in our spirit.... We need to learn to exercise our spirit. Exercising our spirit is like breathing. Even when we are resting we are still breathing.... Just as we breathe without ceasing, we need to pray unceasingly (1 Thes. 5:17). Every time we pray we need to pray in our spirit (Eph. 6:18).

In our spiritual breathing by the exercise of our spirit, we enjoy, receive, and absorb the divine substance with the divine essence, the divine element, and the divine expression. This will cause us to be deified, that is, to be constituted with the processed Triune God to be made God in life and in nature but not in the Godhead. In this sense we may speak of the deification of the believers, a process that will consummate in the New Jerusalem.

The New Jerusalem is a composition of God's chosen, redeemed, regenerated, sanctified, transformed, and glorified people who have been deified. On God's side, the Triune God has been incarnated to be a man; on our side, we are being deified, constituted with the processed and consummated Triune God so that we may be made God in life and in nature to be His corporate expression for eternity. This is the highest truth, and this is the highest gospel. (*Life-study of Job,* pp. 121-122)

Further Reading: Life-study of 1 & 2 Samuel, msgs. 26, 28; *Life-study of Job,* msg. 22; *The Application of the Interpretation of the New Jerusalem to the Seeking Believers,* msgs. 3, 5; *Elders' Training, Book 2: The Vision of the Lord's Recovery,* ch. 6

Enlightenment and inspiration: _____

WEEK 12 — DAY 6

Morning Nourishment

Eph. That He would grant you, according to the riches of
3:16-17 His glory, to be strengthened with power through His Spirit into the inner man, that Christ may make His home in your hearts through faith...
19 ...That you may be filled unto all the fullness of God.

The New Testament verse that best indicates that Christ is building Himself into us is Ephesians 3:17. Here Paul says that Christ is making His home in our hearts. This is building. What is of crucial importance today is the question concerning how much of Christ has been built into us. How much has Christ been built not only into your spirit but into your heart in order to make His home there?

Our spirit, the central part of our being, is surrounded by our heart, which is composed mainly of our mind, emotion, and will. Christ is in our spirit, but how much has Christ made His home in our heart? Most of our hearts are still vacant, not occupied, saturated, and soaked with Christ. Every day our hearts are filled with other things. As a result, Christ is imprisoned in our spirit.

Ephesians 3 indicates strongly that the Triune God is building Himself into us in Christ's making us His home. Paul bowed his knees to the Father and prayed that He would grant us, according to the riches of His glory, to be strengthened with power through His Spirit into the inner man (vv. 14, 16) so that Christ may make His home in our hearts. Here we have the Divine Trinity: the Father is the One to whom Paul prayed; the Spirit is the One who carries out the strengthening; and Christ the Son is the One who is making His home in our heart. By building Himself into our being, He makes our heart, our intrinsic constitution, His home. (*Life-study of 1 & 2 Samuel*, pp. 161-162)

Today's Reading

As we preach the gospel, we should not only tell people that they are sinners, that they are condemned, and that they are going to perish. We have to preach the gospel in a much higher way, telling people that God is calling them to believe in His firstborn Son that they might become His brothers, even His partners in fulfilling God's eternal plan.

God's gospel is to make people holy brothers. This is...revealed in the book of Hebrews. In His resurrection, Christ has made all of us His brothers, and He has come into us to declare the Father to us. Now, as the Sanctifier, He is qualified to perform the sanctifying work that makes us holy. We are His holy brothers and His partners, sharing His anointing for the fulfilling of God's plan.... The world needs to hear these glad tidings. Many thoughtful people in the leading universities throughout the country are wondering about the meaning of human life. So many are asking themselves, "What is the purpose of life? What will happen after my graduation?" No one in the universities can tell them. We must go and tell them the real meaning of life. Go and tell them that they can be the holy brothers of the firstborn Son of God. If the Lord delays His coming back, I hope that after a few years this kind of preaching will be prevailing in all the universities in the United States.

The United States, Europe, and all the leading countries need to hear the higher preaching of such a full gospel, the gospel that produces holy brothers of the firstborn Son of God. If the young people will take up this burden and go to the campuses preaching this gospel, a good number of thoughtful young people will be caught. They will be satisfied. I hope that many of you reading this message will make a deal with the Lord, telling Him that you are willing to be burdened for the preaching of the high gospel. If you are burdened to preach the high gospel, I believe that the Lord will honor your preaching. "Lord, we need more young preachers, more preachers of the fullest gospel!"...Today's world needs a crusade with the preaching of the highest and fullest gospel. (*Life-study of Hebrews,* pp. 155-157).

Further Reading: Life-study of 1 & 2 Samuel, msgs. 24, 29-30; *Life-study of Hebrews,* msg. 14

Enlightenment and inspiration: _____

WEEK 12 — HYMN

Hymns, #948

1. Myst'ry hid from ages now revealed to me,
   'Tis the Christ of God's reality.
   He embodies God, and He is life to me,
   And the glory of my hope He'll be.

   Glory, glory, Christ is life in me!
   Glory, glory, what a hope is He!
   Now within my spirit He's the mystery!
   Then the glory He will be to me.

2. In my spirit He regenerated me,
   In my soul He's now transforming me.
   He will change my body like unto His own,
   Wholly making me the same as He.

3. Now in life and nature He is one with me;
   Then in Him, the glory, I will be;
   I'll enjoy His presence for eternity
   With Him in complete conformity.

WEEK 12 — PROPHECY

Composition for prophecy with main point and sub-points: ___

Reading Schedule for the Recovery Version of the Old Testament with Footnotes

Wk.	Lord's Day	Monday	Tuesday	Wednesday	Thursday	Friday	Saturday
1	☐ Gen 1:1-5	☐ 1:6-23	☐ 1:24-31	☐ 2:1-9	☐ 2:10-25	☐ 3:1-13	☐ 3:14-24
2	☐ 4:1-26	☐ 5:1-32	☐ 6:1-22	☐ 7:1—8:3	☐ 8:4-22	☐ 9:1-29	☐ 10:1-32
3	☐ 11:1-32	☐ 12:1-20	☐ 13:1-18	☐ 14:1-24	☐ 15:1-21	☐ 16:1-16	☐ 17:1-27
4	☐ 18:1-33	☐ 19:1-38	☐ 20:1-18	☐ 21:1-34	☐ 22:1-24	☐ 23:1—24:27	☐ 24:28-67
5	☐ 25:1-34	☐ 26:1-35	☐ 27:1-46	☐ 28:1-22	☐ 29:1-35	☐ 30:1-43	☐ 31:1-55
6	☐ 32:1-32	☐ 33:1—34:31	☐ 35:1-29	☐ 36:1-43	☐ 37:1-36	☐ 38:1—39:23	☐ 40:1—41:13
7	☐ 41:14-57	☐ 42:1-38	☐ 43:1-34	☐ 44:1-34	☐ 45:1-28	☐ 46:1-34	☐ 47:1-31
8	☐ 48:1-22	☐ 49:1-15	☐ 49:16-33	☐ 50:1-26	☐ Exo 1:1-22	☐ 2:1-25	☐ 3:1-22
9	☐ 4:1-31	☐ 5:1-23	☐ 6:1-30	☐ 7:1-25	☐ 8:1-32	☐ 9:1-35	☐ 10:1-29
10	☐ 11:1-10	☐ 12:1-14	☐ 12:15-36	☐ 12:37-51	☐ 13:1-22	☐ 14:1-31	☐ 15:1-27
11	☐ 16:1-36	☐ 17:1-16	☐ 18:1-27	☐ 19:1-25	☐ 20:1-26	☐ 21:1-36	☐ 22:1-31
12	☐ 23:1-33	☐ 24:1-18	☐ 25:1-22	☐ 25:23-40	☐ 26:1-14	☐ 26:15-37	☐ 27:1-21
13	☐ 28:1-21	☐ 28:22-43	☐ 29:1-21	☐ 29:22-46	☐ 30:1-10	☐ 30:11-38	☐ 31:1-17
14	☐ 31:18—32:35	☐ 33:1-23	☐ 34:1-35	☐ 35:1-35	☐ 36:1-38	☐ 37:1-29	☐ 38:1-31
15	☐ 39:1-43	☐ 40:1-38	☐ Lev 1:1-17	☐ 2:1-16	☐ 3:1-17	☐ 4:1-35	☐ 5:1-19
16	☐ 6:1-30	☐ 7:1-38	☐ 8:1-36	☐ 9:1-24	☐ 10:1-20	☐ 11:1-47	☐ 12:1-8
17	☐ 13:1-28	☐ 13:29-59	☐ 14:1-18	☐ 14:19-32	☐ 14:33-57	☐ 15:1-33	☐ 16:1-17
18	☐ 16:18-34	☐ 17:1-16	☐ 18:1-30	☐ 19:1-37	☐ 20:1-27	☐ 21:1-24	☐ 22:1-33
19	☐ 23:1-22	☐ 23:23-44	☐ 24:1-23	☐ 25:1-23	☐ 25:24-55	☐ 26:1-24	☐ 26:25-46
20	☐ 27:1-34	☐ Num 1:1-54	☐ 2:1-34	☐ 3:1-51	☐ 4:1-49	☐ 5:1-31	☐ 6:1-27
21	☐ 7:1-41	☐ 7:42-88	☐ 7:89—8:26	☐ 9:1-23	☐ 10:1-36	☐ 11:1-35	☐ 12:1—13:33
22	☐ 14:1-45	☐ 15:1-41	☐ 16:1-50	☐ 17:1—18:7	☐ 18:8-32	☐ 19:1-22	☐ 20:1-29
23	☐ 21:1-35	☐ 22:1-41	☐ 23:1-30	☐ 24:1-25	☐ 25:1-18	☐ 26:1-65	☐ 27:1-23
24	☐ 28:1-31	☐ 29:1-40	☐ 30:1—31:24	☐ 31:25-54	☐ 32:1-42	☐ 33:1-56	☐ 34:1-29
25	☐ 35:1-34	☐ 36:1-13	☐ Deut 1:1-46	☐ 2:1-37	☐ 3:1-29	☐ 4:1-49	☐ 5:1-33
26	☐ 6:1—7:26	☐ 8:1-20	☐ 9:1-29	☐ 10:1-22	☐ 11:1-32	☐ 12:1-32	☐ 13:1—14:21

Reading Schedule for the Recovery Version of the Old Testament with Footnotes

Wk.	Lord's Day	Monday	Tuesday	Wednesday	Thursday	Friday	Saturday
27	☐ 14:22—15:23	☐ 16:1-22	☐ 17:1—18:8	☐ 18:9—19:21	☐ 20:1—21:17	☐ 21:18—22:30	☐ 23:1-25
28	☐ 24:1-22	☐ 25:1-19	☐ 26:1-19	☐ 27:1-26	☐ 28:1-68	☐ 29:1-29	☐ 30:1—31:29
29	☐ 31:30—32:52	☐ 33:1-29	☐ 34:1-12	☐ Josh 1:1-18	☐ 2:1-24	☐ 3:1-17	☐ 4:1-24
30	☐ 5:1-15	☐ 6:1-27	☐ 7:1-26	☐ 8:1-35	☐ 9:1-27	☐ 10:1-43	☐ 11:1—12:24
31	☐ 13:1-33	☐ 14:1—15:63	☐ 16:1—18:28	☐ 19:1-51	☐ 20:1—21:45	☐ 22:1-34	☐ 23:1—24:33
32	☐ Judg 1:1-36	☐ 2:1-23	☐ 3:1-31	☐ 4:1-24	☐ 5:1-31	☐ 6:1-40	☐ 7:1-25
33	☐ 8:1-35	☐ 9:1-57	☐ 10:1—11:40	☐ 12:1—13:25	☐ 14:1—15:20	☐ 16:1-31	☐ 17:1—18:31
34	☐ 19:1-30	☐ 20:1-48	☐ 21:1-25	☐ Ruth 1:1-22	☐ 2:1-23	☐ 3:1-18	☐ 4:1-22
35	☐ 1 Sam 1:1-28	☐ 2:1-36	☐ 3:1—4:22	☐ 5:1—6:21	☐ 7:1—8:22	☐ 9:1-27	☐ 10:1—11:15
36	☐ 12:1—13:23	☐ 14:1-52	☐ 15:1-35	☐ 16:1-23	☐ 17:1-58	☐ 18:1-30	☐ 19:1-24
37	☐ 20:1-42	☐ 21:1—22:23	☐ 23:1—24:22	☐ 25:1-44	☐ 26:1-25	☐ 27:1—28:25	☐ 29:1—30:31
38	☐ 31:1-13	☐ 2 Sam 1:1-27	☐ 2:1-32	☐ 3:1-39	☐ 4:1—5:25	☐ 6:1-23	☐ 7:1-29
39	☐ 8:1—9:13	☐ 10:1—11:27	☐ 12:1-31	☐ 13:1-39	☐ 14:1-33	☐ 15:1—16:23	☐ 17:1—18:33
40	☐ 19:1-43	☐ 20:1—21:22	☐ 22:1-51	☐ 23:1-39	☐ 24:1-25	☐ 1 Kings 1:1-19	☐ 1:20-53
41	☐ 2:1-46	☐ 3:1-28	☐ 4:1-34	☐ 5:1—6:38	☐ 7:1-22	☐ 7:23-51	☐ 8:1-36
42	☐ 8:37-66	☐ 9:1-28	☐ 10:1-29	☐ 11:1-43	☐ 12:1-33	☐ 13:1-34	☐ 14:1-31
43	☐ 15:1-34	☐ 16:1—17:24	☐ 18:1-46	☐ 19:1-21	☐ 20:1-43	☐ 21:1—22:53	☐ 2 Kings 1:1-18
44	☐ 2:1—3:27	☐ 4:1-44	☐ 5:1—6:33	☐ 7:1-20	☐ 8:1-29	☐ 9:1-37	☐ 10:1-36
45	☐ 11:1—12:21	☐ 13:1—14:29	☐ 15:1-38	☐ 16:1-20	☐ 17:1-41	☐ 18:1-37	☐ 19:1-37
46	☐ 20:1—21:26	☐ 22:1-20	☐ 23:1-37	☐ 24:1—25:30	☐ 1 Chron 1:1-54	☐ 2:1—3:24	☐ 4:1—5:26
47	☐ 6:1-81	☐ 7:1-40	☐ 8:1-40	☐ 9:1-44	☐ 10:1—11:47	☐ 12:1-40	☐ 13:1—14:17
48	☐ 15:1—16:43	☐ 17:1-27	☐ 18:1—19:19	☐ 20:1—21:30	☐ 22:1—23:32	☐ 24:1—25:31	☐ 26:1-32
49	☐ 27:1-34	☐ 28:1—29:30	☐ 2 Chron 1:1-17	☐ 2:1—3:17	☐ 4:1—5:14	☐ 6:1-42	☐ 7:1—8:18
50	☐ 9:1—10:19	☐ 11:1—12:16	☐ 13:1—15:19	☐ 16:1—17:19	☐ 18:1—19:11	☐ 20:1-37	☐ 21:1—22:12
51	☐ 23:1—24:27	☐ 25:1—26:23	☐ 27:1—28:27	☐ 29:1-36	☐ 30:1—31:21	☐ 32:1-33	☐ 33:1—34:33
52	☐ 35:1—36:23	☐ Ezra 1:1-11	☐ 2:1-70	☐ 3:1—4:24	☐ 5:1—6:22	☐ 7:1-28	☐ 8:1-36

Reading Schedule for the Recovery Version of the Old Testament with Footnotes

Wk.	Lord's Day	Monday	Tuesday	Wednesday	Thursday	Friday	Saturday
53	9:1—10:44	Neh 1:1-11	2:1—3:32	4:1—5:19	6:1-19	7:1-73	8:1-18
54	9:1-20	9:21-38	10:1—11:36	12:1-47	13:1-31	Esth 1:1-22	2:1—3:15
55	4:1—5:14	6:1—7:10	8:1-17	9:1—10:3	Job 1:1-22	2:1—3:26	4:1—5:27
56	6:1—7:21	8:1—9:35	10:1—11:20	12:1—13:28	14:1—15:35	16:1—17:16	18:1—19:29
57	20:1—21:34	22:1—23:17	24:1—25:6	26:1—27:23	28:1—29:25	30:1—31:40	32:1—33:33
58	34:1—35:16	36:1-33	37:1-24	38:1-41	39:1-30	40:1-24	41:1-34
59	42:1-17	Psa 1:1-6	2:1—3:8	4:1—6:10	7:1—8:9	9:1—10:18	11:1—15:5
60	16:1—17:15	18:1-50	19:1—21:13	22:1-31	23:1—24:10	25:1—27:14	28:1—30:12
61	31:1—32:11	33:1—34:22	35:1—36:12	37:1-40	38:1—39:13	40:1—41:13	42:1—43:5
62	44:1-26	45:1-17	46:1—48:14	49:1—50:23	51:1—52:9	53:1—55:23	56:1—58:11
63	59:1—61:8	62:1—64:10	65:1—67:7	68:1-35	69:1—70:5	71:1—72:20	73:1—74:23
64	75:1—77:20	78:1-72	79:1—81:16	82:1—84:12	85:1—87:7	88:1—89:52	90:1—91:16
65	92:1—94:23	95:1—97:12	98:1—101:8	102:1—103:22	104:1—105:45	106:1-48	107:1-43
66	108:1—109:31	110:1—112:10	113:1—115:18	116:1—118:29	119:1-32	119:33-72	119:73-120
67	119:121-176	120:1—124:8	125:1—128:6	129:1—132:18	133:1—135:21	136:1—138:8	139:1—140:13
68	141:1—144:15	145:1—147:20	148:1—150:6	Prov 1:1-33	2:1—3:35	4:1—5:23	6:1-35
69	7:1—8:36	9:1—10:32	11:1—12:28	13:1—14:35	15:1-33	16:1-33	17:1-28
70	18:1-24	19:1—20:30	21:1—22:29	23:1-35	24:1—25:28	26:1—27:27	28:1—29:27
71	30:1-33	31:1-31	Eccl 1:1-18	2:1—3:22	4:1—5:20	6:1—7:29	8:1—9:18
72	10:1—11:10	12:1-14	S.S 1:1-8	1:9-17	2:1-17	3:1-11	4:1-8
73	4:9-16	5:1-16	6:1-13	7:1-13	8:1-14	Isa 1:1-11	1:12-31
74	2:1-22	3:1-26	4:1-6	5:1-30	6:1-13	7:1-25	8:1-22
75	9:1-21	10:1-34	11:1—12:6	13:1-22	14:1-14	14:15-32	15:1—16:14
76	17:1—18:7	19:1-25	20:1—21:17	22:1-25	23:1-18	24:1-23	25:1-12
77	26:1-21	27:1-13	28:1-29	29:1-24	30:1-33	31:1—32:20	33:1-24
78	34:1-17	35:1-10	36:1-22	37:1-38	38:1—39:8	40:1-31	41:1-29

Reading Schedule for the Recovery Version of the Old Testament with Footnotes

Wk.	Lord's Day	Monday	Tuesday	Wednesday	Thursday	Friday	Saturday
79	42:1-25	43:1-28	44:1-28	45:1-25	46:1-13	47:1-15	48:1-22
80	49:1-13	49:14-26	50:1—51:23	52:1-15	53:1-12	54:1-17	55:1-13
81	56:1-12	57:1-21	58:1-14	59:1-21	60:1-22	61:1-11	62:1-12
82	63:1-19	64:1-12	65:1-25	66:1-24	Jer 1:1-19	2:1-19	2:20-37
83	3:1-25	4:1-31	5:1-31	6:1-30	7:1-34	8:1-22	9:1-26
84	10:1-25	11:1—12:17	13:1-27	14:1-22	15:1-21	16:1—17:27	18:1-23
85	19:1—20:18	21:1—22:30	23:1-40	24:1—25:38	26:1—27:22	28:1—29:32	30:1-24
86	31:1-23	31:24-40	32:1-44	33:1-26	34:1-22	35:1-19	36:1-32
87	37:1-21	38:1-28	39:1—40:16	41:1—42:22	43:1—44:30	45:1—46:28	47:1—48:16
88	48:17-47	49:1-22	49:23-39	50:1-27	50:28-46	51:1-27	51:28-64
89	52:1-34	Lam 1:1-22	2:1-22	3:1-39	3:40-66	4:1-22	5:1-22
90	Ezek 1:1-14	1:15-28	2:1—3:27	4:1—5:17	6:1—7:27	8:1—9:11	10:1—11:25
91	12:1—13:23	14:1—15:8	16:1-63	17:1—18:32	19:1-14	20:1-49	21:1-32
92	22:1-31	23:1-49	24:1-27	25:1—26:21	27:1-36	28:1-26	29:1—30:26
93	31:1—32:32	33:1-33	34:1-31	35:1—36:21	36:22-38	37:1-28	38:1—39:29
94	40:1-27	40:28-49	41:1-26	42:1—43:27	44:1-31	45:1-25	46:1-24
95	47:1-23	48:1-35	Dan 1:1-21	2:1-30	2:31-49	3:1-30	4:1-37
96	5:1-31	6:1-28	7:1-12	7:13-28	8:1-27	9:1-27	10:1-21
97	11:1-22	11:23-45	12:1-13	Hosea 1:1-11	2:1-23	3:1—4:19	5:1-15
98	6:1-11	7:1-16	8:1-14	9:1-17	10:1-15	11:1-12	12:1-14
99	13:1—14:9	Joel 1:1-20	2:1-16	2:17-32	3:1-21	Amos 1:1-15	2:1-16
100	3:1-15	4:1—5:27	6:1—7:17	8:1—9:15	Obad 1-21	Jonah 1:1-17	2:1—4:11
101	Micah 1:1-16	2:1—3:12	4:1—5:15	6:1—7:20	Nahum 1:1-15	2:1—3:19	Hab 1:1-17
102	2:1-20	3:1-19	Zeph 1:1-18	2:1-15	3:1-20	Hag 1:1-15	2:1-23
103	Zech 1:1-21	2:1-13	3:1-10	4:1-14	5:1—6:15	7:1—8:23	9:1-17
104	10:1—11:17	12:1—13:9	14:1-21	Mal 1:1-14	2:1-17	3:1-18	4:1-6

Reading Schedule for the Recovery Version of the New Testament with Footnotes

Wk.	Lord's Day	Monday	Tuesday	Wednesday	Thursday	Friday	Saturday
1	Matt 1:1-2	1:3-7	1:8-17	1:18-25	2:1-23	3:1-6	3:7-17
2	4:1-11	4:12-25	5:1-4	5:5-12	5:13-20	5:21-26	5:27-48
3	6:1-8	6:9-18	6:19-34	7:1-12	7:13-29	8:1-13	8:14-22
4	8:23-34	9:1-13	9:14-17	9:18-34	9:35—10:5	10:6-25	10:26-42
5	11:1-15	11:16-30	12:1-14	12:15-32	12:33-42	12:43—13:2	13:3-12
6	13:13-30	13:31-43	13:44-58	14:1-13	14:14-21	14:22-36	15:1-20
7	15:21-31	15:32-39	16:1-12	16:13-20	16:21-28	17:1-13	17:14-27
8	18:1-14	18:15-22	18:23-35	19:1-15	19:16-30	20:1-16	20:17-34
9	21:1-11	21:12-22	21:23-32	21:33-46	22:1-22	22:23-33	22:34-46
10	23:1-12	23:13-39	24:1-14	24:15-31	24:32-51	25:1-13	25:14-30
11	25:31-46	26:1-16	26:17-35	26:36-46	26:47-64	26:65-75	27:1-26
12	27:27-44	27:45-56	27:57—28:15	28:16-20	Mark 1:1	1:2-6	1:7-13
13	1:14-28	1:29-45	2:1-12	2:13-28	3:1-19	3:20-35	4:1-25
14	4:26-41	5:1-20	5:21-43	6:1-29	6:30-56	7:1-23	7:24-37
15	8:1-26	8:27—9:1	9:2-29	9:30-50	10:1-16	10:17-34	10:35-52
16	11:1-16	11:17-33	12:1-27	12:28-44	13:1-13	13:14-37	14:1-26
17	14:27-52	14:53-72	15:1-15	15:16-47	16:1-8	16:9-20	Luke 1:1-4
18	1:5-25	1:26-46	1:47-56	1:57-80	2:1-8	2:9-20	2:21-39
19	2:40-52	3:1-20	3:21-38	4:1-13	4:14-30	4:31-44	5:1-26
20	5:27—6:16	6:17-38	6:39-49	7:1-17	7:18-23	7:24-35	7:36-50
21	8:1-15	8:16-25	8:26-39	8:40-56	9:1-17	9:18-26	9:27-36
22	9:37-50	9:51-62	10:1-11	10:12-24	10:25-37	10:38-42	11:1-13
23	11:14-26	11:27-36	11:37-54	12:1-12	12:13-21	12:22-34	12:35-48
24	12:49-59	13:1-9	13:10-17	13:18-30	13:31—14:6	14:7-14	14:15-24
25	14:25-35	15:1-10	15:11-21	15:22-32	16:1-13	16:14-22	16:23-31
26	17:1-19	17:20-37	18:1-14	18:15-30	18:31-43	19:1-10	19:11-27

Reading Schedule for the Recovery Version of the New Testament with Footnotes

Wk.	Lord's Day	Monday	Tuesday	Wednesday	Thursday	Friday	Saturday
27	Luke 19:28-48	20:1-19	20:20-38	20:39—21:4	21:5-27	21:28-38	22:1-20
28	22:21-38	22:39-54	22:55-71	23:1-43	23:44-56	24:1-12	24:13-35
29	24:36-53	John 1:1-13	1:14-18	1:19-34	1:35-51	2:1-11	2:12-22
30	2:23—3:13	3:14-21	3:22-36	4:1-14	4:15-26	4:27-42	4:43-54
31	5:1-16	5:17-30	5:31-47	6:1-15	6:16-31	6:32-51	6:52-71
32	7:1-9	7:10-24	7:25-36	7:37-52	7:53—8:11	8:12-27	8:28-44
33	8:45-59	9:1-13	9:14-34	9:35—10:9	10:10-30	10:31—11:4	11:5-22
34	11:23-40	11:41-57	12:1-11	12:12-24	12:25-36	12:37-50	13:1-11
35	13:12-30	13:31-38	14:1-6	14:7-20	14:21-31	15:1-11	15:12-27
36	16:1-15	16:16-33	17:1-5	17:6-13	17:14-24	17:25—18:11	18:12-27
37	18:28-40	19:1-16	19:17-30	19:31-42	20:1-13	20:14-18	20:19-22
38	20:23-31	21:1-14	21:15-22	21:23-25	Acts 1:1-8	1:9-14	1:15-26
39	2:1-13	2:14-21	2:22-36	2:37-41	2:42-47	3:1-18	3:19—4:22
40	4:23-37	5:1-16	5:17-32	5:33-42	6:1—7:1	7:2-29	7:30-60
41	8:1-13	8:14-25	8:26-40	9:1-19	9:20-43	10:1-16	10:17-33
42	10:34-48	11:1-18	11:19-30	12:1-25	13:1-12	13:13-43	13:44—14:5
43	14:6-28	15:1-12	15:13-34	15:35—16:5	16:6-18	16:19-40	17:1-18
44	17:19-34	18:1-17	18:18-28	19:1-20	19:21-41	20:1-12	20:13-38
45	21:1-14	21:15-26	21:27-40	22:1-21	22:22-29	22:30—23:11	23:12-15
46	23:16-30	23:31—24:21	24:22—25:5	25:6-27	26:1-13	26:14-32	27:1-26
47	27:27—28:10	28:11-22	28:23-31	Rom 1:1-2	1:3-7	1:8-17	1:18-25
48	1:26—2:10	2:11-29	3:1-20	3:21-31	4:1-12	4:13-25	5:1-11
49	5:12-17	5:18—6:5	6:6-11	6:12-23	7:1-12	7:13-25	8:1-2
50	8:3-6	8:7-13	8:14-25	8:26-39	9:1-18	9:19—10:3	10:4-15
51	10:16—11:10	11:11-22	11:23-36	12:1-3	12:4-21	13:1-14	14:1-12
52	14:13-23	15:1-13	15:14-33	16:1-5	16:6-24	16:25-27	1 Cor 1:1-4

Reading Schedule for the Recovery Version of the New Testament with Footnotes

Wk.	Lord's Day	Monday	Tuesday	Wednesday	Thursday	Friday	Saturday
53	1 Cor 1:5-9	1:10-17	1:18-31	2:1-5	2:6-10	2:11-16	3:1-9
54	3:10-13	3:14-23	4:1-9	4:10-21	5:1-13	6:1-11	6:12-20
55	7:1-16	7:17-24	7:25-40	8:1-13	9:1-15	9:16-27	10:1-4
56	10:5-13	10:14-33	11:1-6	11:7-16	11:17-26	11:27-34	12:1-11
57	12:12-22	12:23-31	13:1-13	14:1-12	14:13-25	14:26-33	14:34-40
58	15:1-19	15:20-28	15:29-34	15:35-49	15:50-58	16:1-9	16:10-24
59	2 Cor 1:1-4	1:5-14	1:15-22	1:23—2:11	2:12-17	3:1-6	3:7-11
60	3:12-18	4:1-6	4:7-12	4:13-18	5:1-8	5:9-15	5:16-21
61	6:1-13	6:14—7:4	7:5-16	8:1-15	8:16-24	9:1-15	10:1-6
62	10:7-18	11:1-15	11:16-33	12:1-10	12:11-21	13:1-10	13:11-14
63	Gal 1:1-5	1:6-14	1:15-24	2:1-13	2:14-21	3:1-4	3:5-14
64	3:15-22	3:23-29	4:1-7	4:8-20	4:21-31	5:1-12	5:13-21
65	5:22-26	6:1-10	6:11-15	6:16-18	Eph 1:1-3	1:4-6	1:7-10
66	1:11-14	1:15-18	1:19-23	2:1-5	2:6-10	2:11-14	2:15-18
67	2:19-22	3:1-7	3:8-13	3:14-18	3:19-21	4:1-4	4:5-10
68	4:11-16	4:17-24	4:25-32	5:1-10	5:11-21	5:22-26	5:27-33
69	6:1-9	6:10-14	6:15-18	6:19-24	Phil 1:1-7	1:8-18	1:19-26
70	1:27—2:4	2:5-11	2:12-16	2:17-30	3:1-6	3:7-11	3:12-16
71	3:17-21	4:1-9	4:10-23	Col 1:1-8	1:9-13	1:14-23	1:24-29
72	2:1-7	2:8-15	2:16-23	3:1-4	3:5-15	3:16-25	4:1-18
73	1 Thes 1:1-3	1:4-10	2:1-12	2:13—3:5	3:6-13	4:1-10	4:11—5:11
74	5:12-28	2 Thes 1:1-12	2:1-17	3:1-18	1 Tim 1:1-2	1:3-4	1:5-14
75	1:15-20	2:1-7	2:8-15	3:1-13	3:14—4:5	4:6-16	5:1-25
76	6:1-10	6:11-21	2 Tim 1:1-10	1:11-18	2:1-15	2:16-26	3:1-13
77	3:14—4:8	4:9-22	Titus 1:1-4	1:5-16	2:1-15	3:1-8	3:9-15
78	Philem 1:1-11	1:12-25	Heb 1:1-2	1:3-5	1:6-14	2:1-9	2:10-18

Reading Schedule for the Recovery Version of the New Testament with Footnotes

Wk.	Lord's Day	Monday	Tuesday	Wednesday	Thursday	Friday	Saturday
79	Heb 3:1-6	3:7-19	4:1-9	4:10-13	4:14-16	5:1-10	5:11—6:3
80	6:4-8	6:9-20	7:1-10	7:11-28	8:1-6	8:7-13	9:1-4
81	9:5-14	9:15-28	10:1-18	10:19-28	10:29-39	11:1-6	11:7-19
82	11:20-31	11:32-40	12:1-2	12:3-13	12:14-17	12:18-26	12:27-29
83	13:1-7	13:8-12	13:13-15	13:16-25	James 1:1-8	1:9-18	1:19-27
84	2:1-13	2:14-26	3:1-18	4:1-10	4:11-17	5:1-12	5:13-20
85	1 Pet 1:1-2	1:3-4	1:5	1:6-9	1:10-12	1:13-17	1:18-25
86	2:1-3	2:4-8	2:9-17	2:18-25	3:1-13	3:14-22	4:1-6
87	4:7-16	4:17-19	5:1-4	5:5-9	5:10-14	2 Pet 1:1-2	1:3-4
88	1:5-8	1:9-11	1:12-18	1:19-21	2:1-3	2:4-11	2:12-22
89	3:1-6	3:7-9	3:10-12	3:13-15	3:16	3:17-18	1 John 1:1-2
90	1:3-4	1:5	1:6	1:7	1:8-10	2:1-2	2:3-11
91	2:12-14	2:15-19	2:20-23	2:24-27	2:28-29	3:1-5	3:6-10
92	3:11-18	3:19-24	4:1-6	4:7-11	4:12-15	4:16—5:3	5:4-13
93	5:14-17	5:18-21	2 John 1:1-3	1:4-9	1:10-13	3 John 1:1-6	1:7-14
94	Jude 1:1-4	1:5-10	1:11-19	1:20-25	Rev 1:1-3	1:4-6	1:7-11
95	1:12-13	1:14-16	1:17-20	2:1-6	2:7	2:8-9	2:10-11
96	2:12-14	2:15-17	2:18-23	2:24-29	3:1-3	3:4-6	3:7-9
97	3:10-13	3:14-18	3:19-22	4:1-5	4:6-7	4:8-11	5:1-6
98	5:7-14	6:1-8	6:9-17	7:1-8	7:9-17	8:1-6	8:7-12
99	8:13—9:11	9:12-21	10:1-4	10:5-11	11:1-4	11:5-14	11:15-19
100	12:1-4	12:5-9	12:10-18	13:1-10	13:11-18	14:1-5	14:6-12
101	14:13-20	15:1-8	16:1-12	16:13-21	17:1-6	17:7-18	18:1-8
102	18:9—19:4	19:5-10	19:11-16	19:17-21	20:1-6	20:7-10	20:11-15
103	21:1	21:2	21:3-8	21:9-13	21:14-18	21:19-21	21:22-27
104	22:1	22:2	22:3-11	22:12-15	22:16-17	22:18-21	

Week 7 — Day 4

Today's verses

Rom. 3:22 Even the righteousness of God through the faith of Jesus Christ to all those who believe, for there is no distinction.

10:8 ..."The word is near you, in your mouth and in your heart," that is, the word of the faith which we proclaim.

17 So faith comes out of hearing, and hearing through the word of Christ.

_____
Date

Week 7 — Day 5

Today's verses

Heb. 11:1 Now faith is the substantiation of things hoped for, the conviction of things not seen.

5-6 By faith Enoch...was not found, because God had translated him. For...he obtained the testimony that he had been well pleasing to God. But without faith it is impossible to be well pleasing to Him, for he who comes forward to God must believe that He is and that He is a rewarder of those who diligently seek Him.

_____
Date

Week 7 — Day 6

Today's verses

Rom. 4:17 ...In the sight of God whom [Abraham] believed, who gives life to the dead and calls the things not being as being.

Matt. 17:20 ...If you have faith like a mustard seed, you will say to this mountain, Move from here to there, and it will move; and nothing will be impossible to you.

_____
Date

Week 7 — Day 1

Today's verses

Rom. 1:16-17 ...The gospel...is the power of God unto salvation to everyone who believes....For the righteousness of God is revealed in it out of faith to faith, as it is written, "But the righteous shall have life and live by faith."

1 Pet. 3:18 For Christ also has suffered once for sins, the Righteous on behalf of the unrighteous, that He might bring you to God...

_____
Date

Week 7 — Day 2

Today's verses

Rom. 4:24-25 ...Jesus our Lord...who was delivered for our offenses and was raised for our justification.

1 John 1:9 If we confess our sins, He is faithful and righteous to forgive us our sins and cleanse us from all unrighteousness.

_____
Date

Week 7 — Day 3

Today's verses

Rom. 5:10 For if we, being enemies, were reconciled to God through the death of His Son, much more we will be saved in His life, having been reconciled.

17 For if, by the offense of the one, death reigned through the one, much more those who receive the abundance of grace and of the gift of righteousness will reign in life through the One, Jesus Christ.

8:29 Because those whom He foreknew, He also predestinated to be conformed to the image of His Son, that He might be the Firstborn among many brothers.

_____
Date

Week 8 — Day 4 Today's verses

Deut. 8:7 For Jehovah your God is bringing you to a good land, a land of waterbrooks, of springs and of fountains, flowing forth in valleys and in mountains.

Col. 1:12 Giving thanks to the Father, who has qualified you for a share of the allotted portion of the saints in the light.

Week 8 — Day 5 Today's verses

Deut. 8:8 A land of wheat and barley and vines and fig trees and pomegranates…

John 12:24 Truly, truly, I say to you, Unless the grain of wheat falls into the ground and dies, it abides alone; but if it dies, it bears much fruit.

Week 8 — Day 6 Today's verses

Deut. 8:8-10 …A land of olive trees with oil and of honey; a land in which you will eat bread without scarcity; you will not lack anything in it; a land whose stones are iron, and from whose mountains you can mine copper. And you shall eat and be satisfied, and you shall bless Jehovah your God for the good land which He has given you.

Date _____

Week 8 — Day 1 Today's verses

Eph. 3:8-11 To me, less than the least of all saints, was this grace given to announce to the Gentiles the unsearchable riches of Christ as the gospel and to enlighten all *that they may see* what the economy of the mystery is…in order that now…the multifarious wisdom of God might be made known through the church, according to the eternal purpose which He made in Christ Jesus our Lord.

Date _____

Week 8 — Day 2 Today's verses

Isa. 40:25 To whom will you liken Me, that I should be compared? says the Holy One.

31 …Those who wait on Jehovah will renew their strength; they will mount up with wings like eagles….

Num. 18:20 And Jehovah said to Aaron, You shall have no inheritance in their land, nor shall you have any portion among them; I am your portion and your inheritance among the children of Israel.

31 …It is your reward in return for your service in the Tent of Meeting.

Date _____

Week 8 — Day 3 Today's verses

Eph. 3:2 If indeed you have heard of the stewardship of the grace of God which was given to me for you.

17-19 …That you…may be full of strength to apprehend with all the saints what the breadth and length and height and depth are and to know the knowledge-surpassing love of Christ, that you may be filled unto all the fullness of God.

Date _____

Week 9 — Day 1 Today's verses

Rom. Now to Him who is able to establish you
6:25 according to my gospel, that is, the proclamation of Jesus Christ, according to the revelation of the mystery, which has been kept in silence in the times of the ages.

Eph. …By revelation the mystery was made
3:3 known to me.…

6:19 And [praying] for me, that utterance may be given to me in the opening of my mouth, to make known in boldness the mystery of the gospel.

Date _____

Week 9 — Day 2 Today's verses

Eph. Making known to us the mystery of His
1:9 will according to His good pleasure, which He purposed in Himself.

3:4 By which, in reading it, you can perceive my understanding in the mystery of Christ.

5:32 This mystery is great, but I speak with regard to Christ and the church.

Date _____

Week 9 — Day 3 Today's verses

Col. The mystery which has been hidden from
1:26-27 the ages and from the generations but now has been manifested to His saints; to whom God willed to make known what are the riches of the glory of this mystery among the Gentiles, which is Christ in you, the hope of glory.

Date _____

Week 9 — Day 4 Today's verses

Col. That their hearts may be comforted, they
2:2 being knit together in love and unto all the riches of the full assurance of understanding, unto the full knowledge of the mystery of God, Christ.

1:15 Who is the image of the invisible God, the Firstborn of all creation.

18 And He is the Head of the Body, the church; He is the beginning, the Firstborn from the dead, that He Himself might have the first place in all things.

Date _____

Week 9 — Day 5 Today's verses

Eph. That in Christ Jesus the Gentiles are fellow
3:6 heirs and fellow members of the Body and fellow partakers of the promise through the gospel.

10-11 In order that now to the rulers and the authorities in the heavenlies the multifarious wisdom of God might be made known through the church, according to the eternal purpose which He made in Christ Jesus our Lord.

Date _____

Week 9 — Day 6 Today's verses

Eph. To me, less than the least of all saints, was
3:8-9 this grace given to announce to the Gentiles the unsearchable riches of Christ as the gospel and to enlighten all *that they may see* what the economy of the mystery is, which throughout the ages has been hidden in God, who created all things.

Date _____

Week 10 — Day 1

Today's verses

Eph. 3:2 If indeed you have heard of the stewardship of the grace of God which was given to me for you.

1 Thes. 1:9 For they themselves report concerning us what kind of entrance we had toward you and how you turned to God from the idols to serve a living and true God.

Date _____

Week 10 — Day 2

Today's verses

Rom. 1:1 Paul, a slave of Christ Jesus, a called apostle, separated unto the gospel of God.
9 For God is my witness, whom I serve in my spirit in the gospel of His Son…

2 Tim. 1:3 I thank God, whom I serve from my forefathers in a pure conscience…

Date _____

Week 10 — Day 3

Today's verses

Rom. 1:1-3 …The gospel of God, which He promised beforehand through His prophets in the holy Scriptures, concerning His Son…

15:16 That I might be a minister of Christ Jesus to the Gentiles, a laboring priest of the gospel of God, in order that the offering of the Gentiles might be acceptable, having been sanctified in the Holy Spirit.

Date _____

Week 10 — Day 4

Today's verses

John 4:23-24 But an hour is coming, and it is now, when the true worshippers will worship the Father in spirit and truthfulness, for the Father also seeks such to worship Him. God is Spirit, and those who worship Him must worship in spirit and truthfulness.

Phil. 3:3 For we are the circumcision, the ones who serve by the Spirit of God and boast in Christ Jesus and have no confidence in the flesh.

Date _____

Week 10 — Day 5

Today's verses

Matt. 3:13-15 …Jesus came…to John to be baptized by him. But John tried to prevent Him, saying, It is I who have need of being baptized by You.…But Jesus answered and said to him, Permit it for now, for it is fitting for us in this way to fulfill all righteousness.…

21:32 For John came to you in the way of righteousness, and you did not believe him, but the tax collectors and the harlots believed him.…

Date _____

Week 10 — Day 6

Today's verses

1 Cor. 15:10 But by the grace of God I am what I am; and His grace unto me did not turn out to be in vain, but, on the contrary, I labored more abundantly than all of them, yet not I but the grace of God which is with me.

58 Therefore, my beloved brothers, be steadfast, immovable, always abounding in the work of the Lord, knowing that your labor is not in vain in the Lord.

Date _____

Week 11 — Day 4   Today's verses

Matt. ...When Jesus was in Bethany, in the
26:6-8 house of Simon the leper, a woman came
to Him, having an alabaster flask of ointment of great value, and she poured *it* on
His head as He reclined *at table*. But
when the disciples saw *it*, they were indignant, saying, Why this waste?

12 For in pouring out this ointment on My
body, she has done *it* for My burial.

Date

Week 11 — Day 5   Today's verses

Mark "...You shall love the Lord your God from
12:30 your whole heart and from your whole
soul and from your whole mind and from
your whole strength."

Col. And He is the Head of the Body, the
1:18 church; He is the beginning, the Firstborn
from the dead, that He Himself might
have the first place in all things.

Eph. Grace be with all those who love our Lord
6:24 Jesus Christ in incorruptibility.

Date

Week 11 — Day 6   Today's verses

Mark She has done what she could; she has
14:8 anointed My body beforehand for the
burial.

Matt. Truly I say to you, Wherever this gospel is
26:13 proclaimed in the whole world, what this
woman has done shall also be told as a
memorial of her.

2 Cor. For the love of Christ constrains us...
5:14

Date

Week 11 — Day 1   Today's verses

Gal. But they only heard this: He who was for-
1:23 merly persecuting us is now announcing
as the gospel the faith which formerly he
ravaged.

2 Tim. I have fought the good fight; I have fin-
4:7 ished the course; I have kept the faith.

1 Tim. Holding faith and a good conscience,
1:19 *concerning* which some, thrusting *these*
away, have become shipwrecked regarding the faith.

Date

Week 11 — Day 2   Today's verses

Gal. ...I make known to you, brothers, *con-*
1:11-12 *cerning* the gospel announced by me, that
it is not according to man. For neither did I
receive it from man, nor was I taught *it*,
but *I received it* through a revelation by
Jesus Christ.

Heb. ...Without faith it is impossible to be well
11:6 pleasing *to Him*, for he who comes forward to God must believe that He is and
that He is a rewarder of those who diligently seek Him.

Date

Week 11 — Day 3   Today's verses

Jude Beloved, while using all diligence to
3 write to you concerning our common salvation, I found it necessary to write to you
and exhort *you* to earnestly contend for
the faith once for all delivered to the
saints.

20 But you, beloved, building up yourselves
upon your most holy faith, praying in the
Holy Spirit.

1 Tim. Holding the mystery of the faith in a pure
3:9 conscience.

Date

Week 12 — Day 4   Today's verses

Rom. 8:28-29 — And we know that all things work together for good to those who love God, to those who are called according to His purpose. Because those whom He foreknew, He also predestinated to be conformed to the image of His Son, that He might be the Firstborn among many brothers.

_____
Date

Week 12 — Day 5   Today's verses

Rom. 8:10-11 — But if Christ is in you, though the body is dead because of sin, the spirit is life because of righteousness. And if the Spirit of the One who raised Jesus from the dead dwells in you, He who raised Christ from the dead will also give life to your mortal bodies through His Spirit who indwells you.

_____
Date

Week 12 — Day 6   Today's verses

Eph. 3:16-17, 19 — That He would grant you, according to the riches of His glory, to be strengthened with power through His Spirit into the inner man, that Christ may make His home in your hearts through faith... ...That you may be filled unto all the fullness of God.

_____
Date

Week 12 — Day 1   Today's verses

Rom. 1:1, 3-4 — Paul, a slave of Christ Jesus, a called apostle, separated unto the gospel of God,... concerning His Son, who came out of the seed of David according to the flesh, who was designated the Son of God...

Isa. 43:6-7 — ...Bring My sons from afar,...everyone who is called by My name, whom I have created, formed, and even made for My glory.

_____
Date

Week 12 — Day 2   Today's verses

2 Sam. 7:12-14 — ...I will raise up your seed after you, which will come forth from your body, and I will establish his kingdom. It is he who will build a house for My name, and I will establish the throne of his kingdom forever. I will be his Father, and he will be My son....

Rom. 1:3-4 — Concerning His Son, who came out of the seed of David according to the flesh, who was designated the Son of God in power according to the Spirit of holiness out of the resurrection of the dead, Jesus Christ our Lord.

_____
Date

Week 12 — Day 3   Today's verses

Rom. 8:29 — Because those whom He foreknew, He also predestinated to be conformed to the image of His Son, that He might be the Firstborn among many brothers.

John 12:24 — ...Unless the grain of wheat falls into the ground and dies, it abides alone; but if it dies, it bears much fruit.

_____
Date